GREAT
BATTLES
THROUGH
THE AGES

BATTLE OF THE BULGE

KOREA 1950:
PUSAN TO CHOSIN

THE THIRD CRUSADE:
RICHARD THE LIONHEARTED vs. SALADIN

SINKING OF THE *BISMARCK*

THE *MONITOR* vs. THE *MERRIMACK*

BATTLE OF ACTIUM

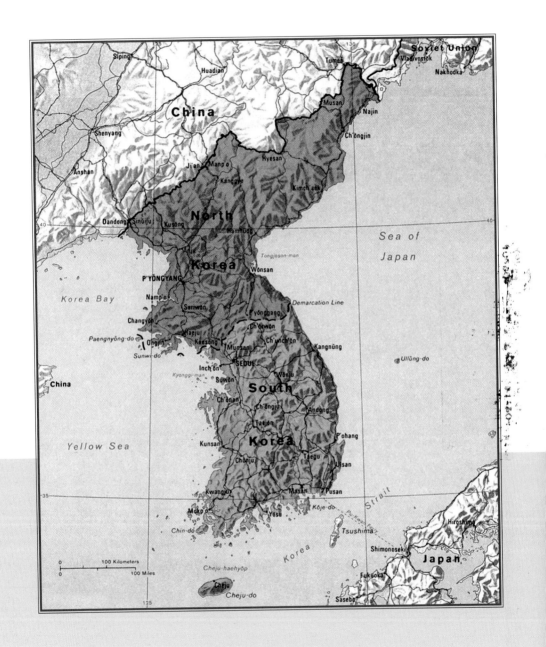

GREAT
BATTLES
THROUGH
THE AGES

KOREA 1950:
PUSAN TO CHOSIN

EARLE RICE JR.

INTRODUCTION BY
CASPAR W. WEINBERGER

CHELSEA HOUSE
PUBLISHERS
A Haights Cross Communications Company
Philadelphia

FRONTIS: A map of the Korean Peninsula and the demarcation line near the 38th parallel.

CHELSEA HOUSE PUBLISHERS

VP, PRODUCT DEVELOPMENT Sally Cheney
DIRECTOR OF PRODUCTION Kim Shinners
CREATIVE MANAGER Takeshi Takahashi
MANUFACTURING MANAGER Diann Grasse

STAFF FOR KOREA 1950: PUSAN TO CHOSIN

EXECUTIVE EDITOR Lee Marcott
SENIOR EDITOR Tara Koellhoffer
PRODUCTION EDITOR Megan Emery
PICTURE RESEARCHER Noelle Nardone
SERIES & COVER DESIGNER Keith Trego
LAYOUT 21st Century Publishing and Communications, Inc.

A Haights Cross Communications Company

http://www.chelseahouse.com

First Printing

1 3 5 7 9 8 6 4 2

Library of Congress Cataloging-in-Publication Data applied for.

ISBN 0-7910-7436-6(HC)   07910-7795-0(PB)

TABLE OF CONTENTS

INTRODUCTION BY CASPAR W. WEINBERGER   6

1   THE SOUND OF THUNDER   11

2   THE ORIGINS OF THE
     KOREAN WAR   19

3   THE FIRST SIX WEEKS   31

4   THE PUSAN PERIMETER   49

5   INCHON   67

6   SEOUL   81

7   CHOSIN   95

8   REMEMBERING THE
     "FORGOTTEN WAR"   111

CHRONOLOGY   116

NOTES   118

BIBLIOGRAPHY   121

FURTHER READING   124

INDEX   125

INTRODUCTION

by Caspar W. Weinberger

There are many ways to study and teach history, which has perhaps been best defined as the "recording and interpretation of past events." Concentration can be on a compilation of major events, or on those events that help prove a theory of the author's. Or the "great man" theory can be applied to write the history of a country or an era, based on a study of the principal leaders or accepted geniuses who are felt to have shaped events that became part of the tapestry of history.

This new Chelsea House series adopts and continues the plan of studying six of the major battles and turning points of wars that did indeed shape much of the history of the periods before, during, and after those wars. By studying the events leading up to major battles and their results, inescapably one learns a great deal about the history of that period.

The first battle, chosen appropriately enough, is the Battle of Actium. There, in 31 B.C., the naval forces of Antony and Cleopatra, and those of Octavian, did battle off the northwest coast of Greece for control of the Roman world. Octavian's victory ended the Roman civil war and gave him unchallenged supremacy, leading to his designation as Augustus, Rome's first emperor. It is highly appropriate that the Battle of Actium be studied first for this series, because the battle was for many decades used as the starting point for a new era.

Next, in chronological order, is a study of the long years of battles between the forces of Richard the Lionhearted and Saladin. This Third Crusade, during the twelfth century, and the various military struggles for Acre and Jerusalem, was the background against which much of the history of modern Britain and Europe and the Middle East was played out.

Coming down to modern times, the series includes a study of the battle that forever changed naval warfare. This battle, the first between two ironclad warships, the *Monitor* and the *Merrimack*, ended the era of naval wars fought by great fleets of sail- or oar-powered ships, with their highly intricate maneuvers. After the *Monitor* and *Merrimack*, all naval battles became floating artillery duels with wholly different tactics and skills required.

The sinking of the German ship *Bismarck* during World War II was not so much a battle as a clear demonstration of the fact that a huge preponderance of naval force on one side could hunt down and destroy one of the most powerful battleships then afloat.

The continued importance of infantry warfare was demonstrated in the Battle of the Bulge, the final attempt of the German army, near the end of World War II, to stave off what in hindsight is now seen as the inevitable victory of the Allies.

The last battle in this series covers the Korean War—one of the most difficult and costly we have fought, and yet a war whose full story is very nearly forgotten by historians and teachers. The story of the Korean War embodies far more than simply the history of a war we fought in the 1950s. It is a history that is dominated by General Douglas MacArthur—but it is also a history of many of the foundation stores of American foreign and domestic policy in the past half century.

These six battles, and the wars of which they were a part, are well worth studying because, although they obviously cannot recount all of history from Actium to Korea, they can and do show the reader the similarities of many of those issues that drive people and governments to war. They also recount the development and changes in technologies by which people have acquired the ability to destroy their fellow creatures ever more effectively and completely.

With the invention and deployment of each new instrument of destruction, from the catapults that were capable of blasting great holes in the walls defending castles and forts, to today's nuclear weapons, the prediction has always been made that the effects and capability of each of those engines of destruction were so awful that their very availability would end war entirely. Thus far, those predictions have always been wrong, although as the full potential of nuclear weapons of mass destruction is increasingly better understood, it may well be that the very nature of these ultimate weapons will, indeed, mean that they will never be used. However, the sheer numbers of these ultimate weapons possessed by many countries, and the possibilities of some of those countries falling under the dictatorship of some of the world's most dangerous leaders, combine to make imaginable a war that could indeed end the world. That is why the United States has expended so much to try to prevent countries such as Iraq and North Korea from continuing to be led by men as inherently dangerous as Saddam Hussein and Kim Il Sung, who are determined to acquire the world's most dangerous weapons.

An increasing knowledge of some of the great battles of the past that have so influenced history is essential unless we want to fulfill the old adage that those who forget history are likely to be condemned to repeat it—with all of its mistakes.

This old adage reminds us also that history is a study not just of great military victories, but also the story of battles lost and the many mistakes that were made by even the greatest of commanders.

After every engagement that involves American troops in action, even on a very small scale, the Pentagon conducts a "Lessons Learned" exercise. What went wrong? What should have been done differently? Did we need more troops, more artillery, more planes? Most important, could more lives of our own troops have been saved?

These mistakes or command errors are not only carefully studied and written about, but they form the basis for war games or exercises in which actual battle situations are refought—sometimes on paper—but frequently with troops reenacting various parts of the combat action. These "lessons learned" exercises become a valuable part of the training of troops and are an even more valuable part of the training of leaders and commanders.

As we can all guess from the short discussions of some of those great battles in this series, there were many opportunities for different commanders and different plans to be used. Indeed, history is perhaps our greatest teacher, and a study of great battles is a great way to learn, even though each battle is different and there will be different lessons to be learned from the post-battle studies.

So, this Chelsea House series serves as a splendid beginning to our study of military history—a history that we must master if we want to see the expansion and success of our basic policy of maintaining peace with freedom.

It is not enough to consider threats to our security and our freedom. We must also be constantly ready to defend our freedom by keeping our ability to prevent any of those threats against us from materializing into real dangers. The study of great battles and how they were won, despite mistakes that have been made, is a vital part of our ability to keep peace with freedom.

BY: Caspar W. Weinberger
Chairman, FORBES Inc.
March 2003

Caspar W. Weinberger was the fifteenth U.S. secretary of defense,
serving under President Ronald Reagan from 1981 to 1987.

The Sound
of Thunder

Soldiers of South Korea's forces were American-trained and believed to be able to resist any North Korean invasion.

North Korean forces, consisting of seven divisions and five brigades, with an air force of 100–150 Soviet-made planes crossed the 38th Parallel at 4 A.M. Korean time, June 25. The main attack was down the Pochon-Uijongbu-Seoul corridor. Other attacks were launched in the Ongjin Peninsula in the west, against Ch'unch'on in the eastern mountains, and down the east coast road. The ROK [Republic of (South) Korea] forces initially available for defense numbered only five divisions with no air force or armor. Ambassador Muccio's report of the attack was received by the State Department [on June 24, 1950] at 9:20 P.M. (EDT).

—Department of State Chronology of Principal Events Relating to the Korean Conflict (quoted in Donald Knox, *The Korean War: Pusan to Chosin*)

Murky, moisture-laden skies ushered in an early darkness in Korea on the night of June 24–25, 1950. By midnight, scattered but heavy rains began descending in sheets upon the fortified positions along the 38th parallel, turning the rich earth slick and releasing the pervasive aroma of human fertilizer from green paddies that checkered much of South Korea's countryside. At an operations post north of the parallel, near a town called Hwach'on, an anxious but self-satisfied smile spread across the square face of 30-year-old Senior Colonel Lee Hak Ku, operations officer of II Corps, North Korean People's Army (NKPA). Relaxing as much as possible in his present circumstances, he lit a cigarette and reflected on the events of the past eight days.

Beginning on June 15, the NKPA had moved every one of its regular divisions into lines of departure along the parallel in just over a week. Some units had been relocated from positions as far north as the Yalu River. Their movements had escaped detection by the South, a remarkable redistribution of forces made possible largely by the good staff work of officers like Senior Colonel Lee. What a great moment! The glorious battle to take back the rest of their country from Syngman Rhee's capitalists was set to begin. Lee lit another cigarette and glanced again at his watch. Only a few more hours to wait.

While Senior Colonel Lee waited anxiously at his post near Hwach'on, Korea, Major General William F. Dean was enjoying himself at a costume party being held at 24th Division headquarters in Kokura, Japan. Dean, the guest of honor, came dressed as a Korean *yangban*, a member of the aristocratic class. A long, flapping robe covered his six-foot, 200-pound frame, but the real attention-getter was the black stovepipe hat perched askew on his close-cropped head. Bill Dean drew rounds of laughter from the 24th Division staff. The general's spouse also came dressed as a

Korean, for both she and her husband had been in the occupation forces in Korea. Dean confessed to her that he felt a bit silly. But on gala occasions a commander owes it to his subordinates to show his human side.

As midnight approached in Seoul, the regular Saturday night dance at the U.S. Korea Military Advisory Group (KMAG) Officers' Open Mess and at least two topflight cocktail parties were in full swing. Among those present at the KMAG club was U.S. Ambassador John J. Muccio, an Italian-born career diplomat. Muccio, a 50-year-old bachelor with jet-black hair, had served in Latin America and enjoyed singing Spanish love songs. Professionally, however, he was dedicated, efficient, and intelligent. On this night of conviviality, though, he was, as usual, the life of the party, despite murmurings of Communist stirrings. In cables to the State Department in May and June 1950, Muccio had described the Republic of Korea Army (ROKA) as "superior" to the NKPA in "training, leadership, morale, marksmanship, and better small arms equipment, especially M-1s [rifles]."[1] If trouble came from the North, the ROKA could handle it.

While the music played on at the KMAG Officers' Open Mess, and the revelry grew noisier, a U.S. brigadier general was relaxing aboard a ship bound for the United States. He had recently completed his tour as KMAG's commander and was heading home on the night of June 24, 1950. Right before he left Korea, the general had told a *Time* magazine reporter, "The South Koreans have the best damn army outside the United States."[2] This was the same army that the Americans had elected to leave unsupported by tanks, heavy guns, and aircraft a year earlier—weaponry not lacking in the arsenal of the North Korean People's Army.

Earlier that month, after observing ROKA maneuvers held by the KMAG commander on June 5, *Time* magazine correspondent Frank Gibney had reported, "Most observers now rate the 100,000-man South Korean army as the best of its size in Asia . . . and no one now believes that the Russian-trained North Korean army could pull off a quick, successful invasion of the South without heavy reinforcements."[3] Gibney did not know that both Korean and Chinese volunteers—veterans of Mao Zedong's Communist armies that had defeated Chiang Kai-shek's Nationalist armies in 1949—were pouring across the Chinese border into North Korea even as he wrote.

Although Muccio and the KMAG commander had expressed concerns to Washington, D.C., in the spring of 1950 that the NKPA's aircraft and tanks might create an imbalance of power in Korea, both men continued to express absolute confidence in the ROK army's ability to repel any invasion from the North. The two men could not have been more wrong.

In Tokyo, Saturday night had crossed over into Sunday morning. At 1:00 A.M., U.S. General of the Army Douglas MacArthur, supreme commander of the Far Eastern Command, was sleeping soundly in his quarters at the U.S. Embassy. For the past two years, he had warned Washington of a potential Communist attack on South Korea, but on Saturday, MacArthur had received no alarming news from Seoul. It had been just another routine day in the Far East.

In Washington, which was 13 hours behind Seoul-Tokyo time, it was almost noon on June 24. Any thought of Korea was among the lesser of President Harry Truman's concerns. With the growing Communist threat on the European continent, Europe and the fate of the young North Atlantic Treaty Organization (NATO), a defense alliance of Western nations, had monopolized his busy calendar for the entire morning. The president was looking forward to spending the rest of the weekend at his home in Missouri.

Three hours later, at his operations post far to the east of

Communist-backed North Korea had the advantage of Soviet equipment such as artillery, aircraft, and tanks, like this Soviet-built T-34.

Seoul, Senior Colonel Lee Hak Ku looked at his watch again, as he had done at five-to-ten-minute intervals for the past several hours. The hour of departure was at last only moments away. All around him Lee could hear the subdued rustlings of young troops in mustard-colored cotton uniforms as they moved into their final attack positions.

At four invasion corridors to the south, diesel engines coughed and shuddered to life on low-slung, wide-tracked Soviet-built T-34 tanks, their clatter largely muffled by a heavy drizzle, all that remained from an earlier torrential monsoon downpour. Artillery commanders checked their preregistered grid coordinates for their preloaded cannons one last time.

At the top of the hour, the big guns broke the silence and the peace. Beginning at the Yellow Sea in the west and exploding eastward toward the Sea of Japan, cannon thunder shook the earth, and flame-spouting muzzles lit up the night skies. The tanks moved out, heading southward along wet but firm roads, their tracks splattering mud on the hordes of small, shrieking men in yellow-brown shirts following close behind.

Open Invitations

Many critics of the Truman administration cite Secretary of State Dean G. Acheson's speech before the National Press Club on January 12, 1950, as an open invitation to Communist North Korea to invade its democratic neighbor to the south. In outlining the U.S. defense perimeter in the Pacific Ocean, Acheson stressed the importance of Japan but omitted Korea from U.S. strategic considerations. The perimeter, as defined by Acheson,

> runs along the Aleutians to Japan and then goes to the Ryukyus [and] from the Ryukyus to the Philippine Islands. . . . So far as the military security of other areas in the Pacific is concerned, it must be clear that no person can guarantee these areas against military attack. But it must also be clear that such a guarantee is hardly sensible or necessary within the realm of practical relationship.*

Five months later, in May 1950, Texas Senator Tom Connally, chairman of the Senate Foreign Relations Committee, said that the United States would not intervene if the Soviets seized South Korea because Korea was not "very greatly important."** Republic of Korea President Syngman Rhee publicly chastised Connally on May 10 for extending "an open invitation for the Communists to come down and take over South Korea."*** Seven weeks later, the Communists did.

* Quoted in Robert Leckie, *Conflict: The History of the Korean War, 1950–53*. New York: Da Capo Press, 1996, p. 37.

** Ibid.

*** Quoted in Sergei N. Goncharov, John W. Lewis, and Xue Litai, *Uncertain Partners: Stalin, Mao, and the Korean War*. Stanford, CA: Stanford University Press, 1993, p. 151.

Lee Hak Ku, eyes ablaze with excitement, shouted, "*Manzai!*"[4] Lee's staff echoed his cry, which in English means merely "Hoorah!" In this setting, however, the word served to express their confidence of victory in the battle to come.

On the southern side of the demarcation line, sentries heard the distant rumble of guns and mistook their sound for monsoon thunderclaps until the shrieking shells began exploding among them. And thus began the conflict that possibly prevented World War III—but at a cost of more than 4 million lives.

It was 4:00 A.M., Sunday, June 25, 1950.

Soviet Premier Joseph Stalin (seen here) was one of the "Big Three" leaders who met first in Yalta and then in Potsdam to determine how the victorious Allies would reorganize Europe after World War II.

The Origins of the Korean War

Korea may appear to offer a tempting opportunity [for Stalin] . . . to strengthen enormously the economic resources of the Soviet Far East, to acquire ice-free ports, and to occupy a dominating strategic position in relation both to China and Japan. . . . A Soviet occupation of Korea would create an entirely new strategic situation in the Far East, and its repercussions within China and Japan might be far reaching.

—State Department paper, October 1943
(quoted in William Stueck, *The Korean War: An International History*)

Worc War II ended with Japan's unconditional surrender on September 2, 1945, but the struggle for world domination was only beginning. The United States and the

Soviet Union, allies during the conflict, emerged from the war as the two strongest nations in the world. They were shortly to become antagonists in a chilling ideological war that pitted capitalism against communism. The conflict was aptly termed the Cold War. Historians and political observers disagree as to precisely when the Cold War began, but a consensus seems to favor the Yalta Conference of 1945 as the time and place of its origin. It was at Yalta, also, that the first steps toward a hot (shooting) war in Korea were taken.

The Yalta Conference was held at a remote Black Sea resort in Crimea on February 4–11, 1945. It brought together the leaders of the "Big Three" Allied powers—the United States, Great Britain, and the Soviet Union—to discuss plans for the postwar world. The respective leaders were U.S. President Franklin D. Roosevelt, British Prime Minister Winston Churchill, and Soviet Premier Joseph Stalin.

The three leaders tentatively agreed on a four-nation occupation of Germany (with France as the fourth power) and on a guarantee of a representative government in Poland. They further agreed to hold a founding confer-ence for the United Nations (UN) later in the year. Most important in regard to Far Eastern affairs, Stalin agreed to enter the war against Japan within three months of Germany's defeat. But the Soviet leader's commitment came with strings attached to it.

Stalin insisted that Outer Mongolia (Mongolian People's Republic) remain under Soviet control without interference from China. He further wanted access to two Chinese ports in Manchuria—Dairen (Dalian) and Port Arthur (Lüshun)—and Soviet joint ownership with China of the Chinese Eastern and Southern Manchurian railroads. And he demanded that the "former rights of Russia violated by the treacherous attack of Japan in 1904"[5] (during the Russo-Japanese War of 1904–1905) be restored, chiefly possession of the southern half of the Sakhalin Peninsula.

It is unclear whether Stalin's diplomacy with Churchill and Truman at the Potsdam Conference, at which this photograph was taken, truly focused on the "reconstruction" of Germany and Japan or whether he was more interested in the "division of spoils" to be had after the war ended.

Roosevelt raised no objections to Stalin's territorial claims on Japan but said that he would support concessions from China only with the approval of Nationalist Chinese leader Chiang Kai-shek (Jiang Jieshi). Stalin, who had once commented, "Sincere diplomacy is no more possible than dry water or iron wood,"[6] accepted this condition and pledged to seek an accord with Chiang.

At the same time, in an effort to allay any American concerns about the future of Korea, Stalin informally agreed with a declaration issued earlier by Roosevelt, Churchill, and Chiang at the Cairo Conference of 1943, which stated that "in due course Korea should be free and independent."[7] In reality, Stalin had already groomed 36 key Korean Communists, either Soviet-born or exiled Koreans, to rule a Korean puppet state that he planned to establish at his southeastern frontier at war's end.

Like the tsars of old Russia, Stalin was obsessed with creating a buffer zone against potential enemies along his nation's far-reaching borders. Commenting on Stalin's diplomatic strategy, Sergei N. Goncharov, John W. Lewis, and Xue Litai, eminent authorities on the Sino-Soviet alliance and the origins of the Korean War, write:

> The security equation for Stalin was simple: subordinate the interests of weak states (including China) to those of the powerful, divide the strategic regions of the world into spheres of influence, and widen the buffer zones along the periphery of the Soviet state. His was the diplomacy of imperial [tsarist] Russia.[8]

After Germany's defeat in May 1945, the Big Three, with a different cast of characters, met again at Potsdam, a suburb of devastated Berlin, Germany, during July 17–August 2, 1945. Although Stalin continued to head the Soviet delegation, former Vice President Harry Truman had replaced Roosevelt, who had died the previous April, and Clement Attlee, Great Britain's newly elected prime minister, took over for Churchill on the second day of the conference.

The Potsdam Conference basically reaffirmed the Yalta agreements, but a peripheral event of major importance occurred on the day before the meeting began: The first atomic bomb was successfully tested by U.S. scientists near Alamogordo, New Mexico. After the day's talks on July 24, as Truman wrote later, he "casually mentioned to Stalin that we had a new weapon of unusual destructive force."[9] Stalin, who already knew about the bomb through espionage channels, appeared unimpressed. Truman, on the other hand, secretly hoped that the American atomic bomb would force the Japanese to surrender before Stalin could honor his vow to enter the war against the Japan. That did not happen.

On August 6, 1945, the United States dropped an atomic bomb on the Japanese port city of Hiroshima. The bomb's destructive force turned out to be far greater than Stalin had anticipated. Two days later, he declared war against Japan and sent troops into Japanese-held Manchuria. The next day, the United States dropped a second atomic bomb on the Japanese city of Nagasaki. Japan informally agreed to accept surrender terms on August 15. Thus, the Soviets, after only a few minor confrontations with a Japanese army stripped of aircraft (to defend Japan's home islands) had reestablished their presence on the Pacific shores and had "earned" their share of the spoils of war in the Far East.

"With the physical presence in northern China of 1.5 million Soviet soldiers, facing the defeated Japanese army," writes Ronald Gregor Suny, professor of political science at the University of Chicago, "the Nationalist Chinese government signed a Treaty of Friendship and Alliance with the USSR [Union of Soviet Socialist Republics, or Soviet Union], agreeing to the concessions in China granted to Stalin at Yalta."[10] All that remained to be settled in the Far East was the postwar status of Korea.

With the Soviet armies rolling across Manchuria and rushing southward toward Korea in August 1945, the big question on American minds became: Where would they stop? Since the Americans and the Soviets had never discussed a joint occupation, they had not established a demarcation line for that purpose.

On the night of August 10–11, an emergency session of the State-War-Navy (departments) Coordinating Committee, held at the Pentagon in Washington, D.C., addressed the U.S. planning lapse. For political reasons, State Department representatives wanted to receive the Japanese surrender in Korea as far north as possible. But Dean Rusk, a young colonel on the staff of Army Chief of Staff General George C.

Marshall, pointed out that the military was "faced with the scarcity of U.S. forces immediately available and time and space factors which would make it difficult to reach very far north before Soviet troops could enter the area."[11] At that point, Assistant Secretary of War John J. McCloy told Colonels Rusk and C.H. Bonesteel III to retire to an anteroom with a map of Korea and decide on a line that would reconcile political wishes with military reality.

"The military view was that if our proposals for receiving the surrender greatly over-reached our probable military capabilities," Rusk observed later, "there would be little likelihood of Soviet acceptance—and speed was the essence of the problem." After conferring, Rusk (who would later serve as secretary of state under Presidents John F. Kennedy and Lyndon B. Johnson) and Bonesteel suggested the 38th parallel of latitude, "even though it was further north than could be realistically reached by U.S. forces in the event of Soviet disagreement."[12]

This 190-mile (306-kilometer) demarcation line across the center of Korea made no sense, either economically or militarily. The two colonels had selected it because they "felt it was important to include the capital of Korea [Seoul] in the area of responsibility of American troops."[13] To the surprise of the Americans, the Soviets accepted the 38th parallel without reservations, and the occupation of Korea commenced.

The Americans had intended for the 38th parallel to provide only a temporary dividing line to facilitate the surrender of Japanese forces. It was arbitrary, imaginary, and never meant to set up two zones of occupation; the Americans and the Soviets had never discussed a joint occupation. The line held no historical or political meaning. Militarily, it posed enormous defensive problems along its 190-mile length, as it sliced straight through mountains at odd angles and crossed 12 rivers, more than 75 streams, eight major highways, several hundred lesser roads, and six north-south rail lines.

Economically, the dividing line made even less sense. The southern sector, populated by some 21 million people in an area of 37,000 square miles, contained 12 of Korea's 20 largest cities, including Seoul, with 2 million people. Primarily agricultural, the region customarily supplied the entire country with rice and other staples. The northern sector, although larger with 48,000 square miles, was inhabited by only about 9 million people. Because of its highly developed hydroelectric plants, the North contained most of Korea's industries—chemical, steel, cement, and fertilizers that complemented the agrarian products of the South. Neither sector could sustain itself independently of the other. One of the few flaws for which the 38th parallel could not be faulted was the climate— sizzling heat in summer and extreme subzero temperatures in winter.

The Korean Peninsula, 450 miles (724 kilometers) long and averaging 160 miles (258 kilometers) in width, roughly resembles the state of Florida but is about half again larger in size. It is bounded by the Yellow Sea in the west, the Sea of Japan in the east, and the Korea Strait in the south. In the north, the Yalu and Tumen rivers separate it from the People's (Communist) Republic of China (PRC) and the Soviet Union. Forests cover much of the peninsula, and the Taebaek mountain range forms a spine that parallels the east coast.

Korea is known as the Land of the Morning Calm. But since the beginning of recorded history, Korea's strategic location at the crossroads of East Asia has destined it to be a perpetual battleground in a constant struggle for dominance in that region. From the second century B.C., Korea has been either self-ruled or variously ruled by the Chinese, the Mongols, and, from 1910 until 1945, the Japanese. The Koreans, a robust people, practice Buddhism and are racially related to the Japanese and Manchurians. Describing the Koreans, popular historian John Toland conjectures:

> It was perhaps their topography and hardy life that made Koreans different from the Chinese and the Japanese. They took pride in their physical endurance, reacted violently to challenge and could be both sweetnatured [sic] and aggressive. Yet even under the most adverse circumstances they retained a sense of humor. They were often called the Irish of the Orient.[14]

After 33 years of Japanese subjugation, the Koreans took heart at the promise of freedom proclaimed by Roosevelt, Churchill, and Chiang Kai-shek at the Cairo Declaration in 1943, and they looked forward to their independence at war's end. But Roosevelt had told Stalin at Yalta that it would take 20 to 30 years before Korea would be ready for total independence. Accordingly, at war's end, Koreans resented the influx of occupation forces on both sides of the 38th parallel.

By the time word of the agreed-upon demarcation line reached the field, scattered Soviet army units had already crossed the parallel and were moving rapidly down the highway toward Seoul. When they learned of the demarcation line, though, they withdrew quickly to positions north of the boundary. Their prompt withdrawal marked the last instance of Soviet-American cooperation in Korea.

In line with Stalin's compulsion to buffer the Soviet Union with friendly nations, the Soviets immediately began to construct permanent fortifications along the "temporary" dividing line in Korea. The Soviets stopped virtually all traffic in and out of the North, severed railway lines, and cut off electric power to the South. Swiftly, and suddenly, almost before the Americans—and the Korean people themselves—could grasp what was happening, there were two Koreas.

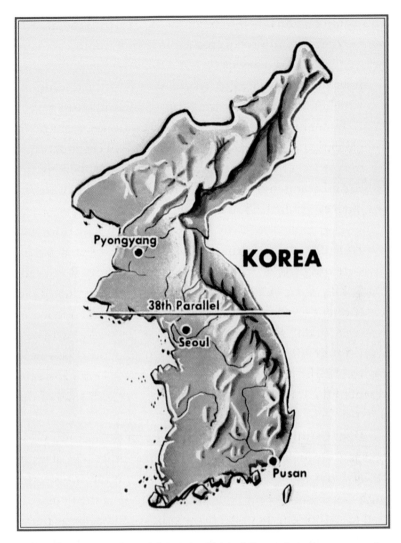

The 38th parallel that ultimately divided Korea into two separate countries was determined as much by convenience as by any political or military strategy.

With the hardening of the Cold War between the United States and the Soviet Union, the temporary division of Korea became more and more permanent. In July 1946, President Truman angrily declared that Korea was "an ideological battleground on which our entire success in Asia depends."[15] After George C. Marshall, now U.S.

secretary of state, failed to reach an accord with the Soviets on the question of Korea, the United States laid the issue before the United Nations (UN)—the world peacekeeping body formed at the close of World War II—for resolution.

The UN General Assembly proposed an all-Korea election, after which all foreign troops were to be withdrawn after the establishment of a legal government. In 1948, after Moscow rejected the UN plan, elections moved ahead in the South and resulted in the creation of the Republic of Korea (ROK) on August 15, 1948, with former revolutionary leader and exile Syngman Rhee as its president. Moscow responded by establishing the Democratic People's Republic of Korea (DPRK) in the North on September 9, 1948, headed by Kim Il Sung. Kim was one of the 36 Korean

Americans Land in Korea

On June 10, 1871, a U.S. force of 109 marines and 542 sailors landed in Korea. They were responding to the massacre of the crew of an American merchant ship by Korean river pirates, and to subsequent gunfire attacks on two American gunboats on the Han River by Korean soldiers.

Led by marine Captain McLane W. Tilton, the landing party attacked three Korean forts along the river approaches to the Korean capital of Chemulpo (later Seoul). In savage hand-to-hand actions, they overwhelmed Korean defenders of the three forts in what became known as the "weekend war." After Irish-born marine Private James Dougherty killed the Korean commander, the party returned victoriously to their ship carrying 13 dead and wounded and three huge Korean flags. Dougherty was one of six marines and nine sailors to win the Medal of Honor during the engagement. Their action in defense of American interests in the Far East had been swift, sure, and decisive.

Seventy-nine years later, American armed forces would return to Korea in defense of South Korea's right to choose democracy over communism. This time, U.S. troops would stay not for a weekend but for three of the bloodiest years in American history.

Communists whom Stalin had groomed to govern the satellite state on his southeastern frontier. Each Korean republic claimed jurisdiction over the entire peninsula.

The Soviet Union, having by then trained and equipped a formidable North Korean army, which was vastly superior to the Republic of Korea Army, began to withdraw its troops from the North and urged the United States to follow suit in the South. The last Soviet troops left North Korea with great fanfare on December 26, 1948. But U.S. occupation forces remained in the South for another six months before withdrawing on June 30, 1949.

Upon their departure, the Americans left behind 500 officers and men of the U.S. Korea Military Advisory Group to complete the training of the ROK Army, which was apparently an impossible mission. President Truman and his chiefs of staff wanted to mold a South Korean army sturdy enough to repel any attack by the NKPA, but not strong enough to launch its own attack on the North. For this reason, the Americans decided not to leave behind any aircraft, tanks, or heavy guns—a decision that would bring grave repercussions 12 months later.

With only a handful of advisors remaining in the South (and likely in the North as well), the armies on both sides of the 38th parallel began shoring up their defenses, with each dedicated to the reunification of the two Koreas. Early in 1950, border clashes erupted between the two antagonists, touching off rumors of an impending invasion of South Korea. In a single week, March 3–10, 18 armed incidents flared up along the parallel, and Communist insurgents staged 29 attacks across the South.

Then suddenly, in May, armed confrontations dropped off sharply and an eerie tranquillity settled over the Land of the Morning Calm as NKPA forces began to mass silently along the 38th parallel. The unearthly calm was about to be shattered.

Kim Il Sung, North Korea's Communist leader, governed the country from 1948 until his death in 1994 at the age of 82. When he was a child, Kim Il Sung's family emigrated to Manchuria (China), where he became indoctrinated in communism. He was forced to leave for the Soviet Union in 1941 and then joined the Soviet Army on its drive into Korea in 1945.

The First Six Weeks

Considering the relative strength and combat readiness of the forces that faced each other across the 38ʰ parallel in June 1950, it was a marvel that the North Korean armies were delayed at all in their drive to overrun all of South Korea.

—General Matthew B. Ridgway (in *The Korean War*)

In the predawn darkness of Sunday, June 25, 1950, the North Korean People's Army, commanded by Marshal Choe Yong Gun and spearheaded by 120 Soviet T-34 medium tanks, carried out a successful surprise attack and quickly overwhelmed the Republic of Korea Army defenders along the 38ᵗʰ parallel. Choe's main force headed next down the west side of the peninsula toward Seoul, while secondary thrusts advanced down the Ongjin Peninsula in the west, toward Chunchon (Ch'unch'on) and Wonju in the central mountains, and down the eastern coastal road toward Samchok, Yongdok, and Pohang (P'ohang).

The ROKA fought bravely. Unfortunately, with many of its soldiers on weekend leave and the remainder under assault by tanks and heavy artillery, the ROKA, without effective countering weaponry, was vastly outnumbered and outgunned and was quickly routed. Only in one small eastern sector, where the defending ROK division was at full strength and the NKPA attacked without tanks, were the South Koreans able to mount a determined resistance.

The government radio in the North Korean capital of Pyongyang (P'yongyang) waited for five and a half hours after the onset of the NKPA attack on South Korea to offer a ridiculous explanation for the outbreak of hostilities. At 9:30 A.M. on June 25, Korean time, the voice of North Korean Premier Kim Il Sung himself proclaimed over the airwaves:

> The South Korean puppet clique has rejected all methods for peaceful reunification proposed by the Democratic People's Republic of Korea and dared to commit armed aggression . . . north of the 38th parallel. The [DPRK] ordered a counterattack to repel the invading troops. The South Korean puppet clique will be held responsible for whatever results may be brought about by this development.[16]

Kim failed to explain why it had been necessary for his troops to have advanced already 10 to 20 miles (16 to 32 kilometers) inside South Korea to "repel" soldiers of the "puppet clique."

Just prior to 9:30 P.M. on June 24 in Washington, shortly

before Kim's broadcast, the State Department had received a cable from Ambassador John J. Muccio that stated:

> North Korea forces invaded Republic of Korea territory at several points this morning. . . . It would appear from the nature of the attack and the manner in which it was launched that it constitutes an all-out offensive against ROK.[17]

Thirty minutes later, the report reached the hands of U.S. Secretary of State Dean G. Acheson. He immediately telephoned President Truman, then spending the weekend at his home in Independence, Missouri. Without enough information to initiate definitive action, the two U.S. leaders agreed to request an emergency meeting of the UN Security Council.

On the afternoon of June 25, the council (minus the Soviets, who had been boycotting since January because the UN refused to recognize Communist China in place of Nationalist China) adopted a U.S.-sponsored resolution that blamed North Korea for a "breach of the peace" and called for the "immediate cessation of hostilities."[18] The resolution also called for a withdrawal of North Korean forces to the 38th parallel. Few informed observers expected the North Koreans to heed the resolution.

The council also called on all members "to render every assistance to the United Nations in the execution of this resolution and to refrain from giving assistance to the North Korean authorities."[19] President Truman interpreted this call for help as a legal justification to intervene in Korea.

When news of the invasion reached General MacArthur, who only five years earlier had accepted Japan's surrender in World War II, he appeared unruffled by North Korea's audacity. "This is probably only a reconnaissance in force," he told reporters. "If Washington will not hobble me, I can handle it with one arm tied behind my back."[20]

That night, Truman, acting independently, dispatched a threefold order to MacArthur in Tokyo, directing the Far East commander to supply the ROK forces with ammunition and equipment, evacuate American dependents from Korea, and survey the situation on the peninsula to learn how best to lend further aid to the South Koreans. Truman also ordered elements of the U.S. 7th Fleet—then operating in the waters off the Philippine and Ryukyu islands—to steam at full speed for Japan.

On June 26, in a broad interpretation of the Security Council's request for "every assistance," Truman authorized MacArthur to use air and naval forces against North Korean targets south of the 38th parallel. The president further directed the bulk of the 7th Fleet to the Formosa (Taiwan) Strait that separated the Chinese Communists on the mainland from the Chinese Nationalists on Formosa to head off any widening of the hostilities by either of the two Chinas.

The next day, after it became clear that North Korea intended to ignore UN demands to withdraw from South Korea, the UN Security Council (again at the urging of the United States) acted in unprecedented fashion, resolving "that the Members of the United Nations furnish such assistance to the Republic of Korea as may be necessary to repel the armed attack and to restore international peace and security in the area."[21] The council's action marked the first time in history that a world body had condemned aggression and then raised an armed force to combat the aggressor.

The United States would bear the largest share of the burden occasioned by the UN pledge to the Republic of South Korea. Ultimately, 22 nations would join the U.S.-led coalition to oust the North Koreans. Sixteen of them would send ground troops. But it would take time for help to reach the embattled peninsula, and time was a commodity of

Strife between Communist forces on mainland China and Chinese Nationalist forces on the island of Formosa was a recurring threat to the peace in Southeast Asia.

which the South Koreans had very little. Seventy-two hours after the start of hostilities—on June 28—the South Korean capital of Seoul fell to Marshal Choe's North Korean invaders.

The next day, General MacArthur flew into Suwon, South Korea, and personally assessed the military situation. According to Russell Brines, Tokyo bureau chief for the Associated Press, one of four correspondents who toured the ROK lines with the Far East commander, they

> drove through the swirling, defeated South Korean army and masses of bewildered, pathetic civilian refugees for a firsthand look at the battlefront. . . . Throughout the journey, the convoy constantly risked enemy air action, against which there was no adequate protection. . . . The crump of mortars was loud and clear, and the North Koreans could have seriously endangered the party with gunfire from only moderately heavy artillery.[22]

At one point during their tour, MacArthur stood on a small mound off a road crammed with retreating soldiers, refugees, and ambulances and viewed the carnage around him. With his hands jammed in his rear trouser pockets and his corncob pipe jutting skyward, he surveyed the destruction outside Seoul. "Only a mile away, I could see the towers of smoke rising from the ruins of this fourteenth-century city," he later wrote. "It was a tragic scene."[23] While standing on that little knoll, as MacArthur would later reveal, he conceived a daring plan for a huge amphibious landing behind the North Koreans. He called it "Operation Blueheart."

When MacArthur returned to Tokyo, he sent a long report to Washington, which ended with this warning:

> Unless provision is made for the full utilization of the Army-Navy-Air team in this shattered area, our mission will at best be needlessly costly in life, money and prestige. At worst, it might even be doomed to failure.[24]

In Washington, President Truman had already queried

the Soviets as to their intentions in Korea. Upon receipt of a vaguely worded reply, he quipped, "That means the Soviets are going to let the Chinese and the North Koreans do the fighting for them."[25] Though he could not know it then with certainty, his off-the-cuff judgment hit the mark squarely.

Moreover, the president now felt sure that the North Koreans intended to drive all the way to the southern tip of the peninsula, after which they would hold a Communist-controlled election to reunify the two Koreas, probably by mid-August. Time was fleeting and fast action imperative. Truman immediately authorized the use of a single U.S. regimental combat team (RCT). Shortly afterward, he added instructions that effectively committed every arm of the U.S. military to action and sanctioned air and naval attacks on all but a few targets north of the 38th parallel. In doing so, he was fulfilling MacArthur's request for "full utilization."

President Truman had agonized over whether to commit U.S. troops to ground action in Korea. He later commented that intervention there had been his toughest decision as president, and he explained that he had acted to check Soviet designs on world domination: "If the Communists were permitted to force their way into the Republic of Korea without opposition from the free world, no small nation would have the courage to resist threats and aggression by stronger Communist neighbors."[26] As the leader of the free world, the United States was putting its prestige at risk.

Congress supported the president's action and voted for a one-year extension to the draft. But since Truman had acted by executive order rather than by asking Congress for a formal declaration of war, Republican Senator Robert A. Taft of Ohio put his protest on the record: "If the incident is permitted to go by without protest, at least from this body, we would have finally terminated for all time the right of Congress to declare war, which is granted to Congress alone by the Constitution of the United States."[27]

Taft's words went unheeded. The president had already established a precedent. No formal declaration of war would be sought for future actions in Vietnam, Grenada, Panama, and the Persian Gulf. In fact, Congress has not exercised its right to declare war since December 8, 1941. If South Korea were to be saved, however, then Truman's unilateral decision to fight had come none too soon.

The North Koreans had already begun a dramatic dash to Pusan. They wanted to overrun the entire peninsula and force the reunification of Korea under Communist rule before external forces could come to the aid of the over-matched South Korean forces. Militarily, invading hostile shores would pose far greater difficulties for the United States than debarking at friendly ports defended by a ROK Army still intact and up to the task. Politically, an attack on a reunified Korea might not rest well with other UN nations, which might be less eager to resurrect a fallen Republic of Korea after the fact.

After one week of war, Syngman Rhee's army, which had begun hostilities with some 98,000 troops, could now account for only 54,000. The rest had scattered to the winds, some never to be seen or heard from again. "South Korean casualties as an index to fighting have not shown adequate resistance capabilities or the will to fight," MacArthur caustically informed Washington, "and our best estimate is that complete collapse is imminent."[28]

The general knew that drastic action would be necessary to stem the Communist advance. He defined his strategy in four words: "Trade space for time." This meant fighting a delaying action to gain sufficient time to land more troops from Japan and bring in heavy weapons, tanks, and supplies. He later explained to Congress that he hoped by an "arrogant display of strength to fool the enemy into the belief that I had a much greater resource at my disposal than I did."[29] When the Americans first engaged the North

Koreans on the battlefield, however, it is probably fair to say that MacArthur's "arrogant display of strength" featured far more arrogance than strength.

At 10:30 P.M. on June 30, Lieutenant Colonel Charles B. "Brad" Smith received a telephone call at his quarters near Kumamoto, Kyushu. The call came from his boss, Colonel Richard W. Stephens, commander of the 21st Infantry Regiment of Major General William F. Dean's 24th Division. Stephens told Smith, "The lid has blown off. Get on your clothes and report to the CP [command post]."[30]

Stephens ordered Smith to put together a task force for movement to Korea. Five and a half hours later, Smith, along with parts of his 1st Battalion, 21st Infantry, 24th Division, and a few other soldiers, was en route by truck to Itazuke air base, 75 miles (121 kilometers) away. At Itazuke, division commander Dean greeted Smith, shook his hand, and explained why he had summoned Smith and his troops.

Under orders from 8th U.S. Army (EUSA) commander Lieutenant General Walton H. Walker to direct a delaying action in Korea, Dean had selected Smith and his small group to fly into Pusan and spearhead the mission. Smith and his troops would soon have the dubious distinction of being the first U.S. ground force to fight in the Korean War. The rest of the 24th Division was to follow by ship from Japan as soon as possible. Dean's orders to Smith were a model of brevity:

> When you get to Pusan, head for Taejon. We want to stop the North Koreans as far from Pusan as we can. Block the main road as far north as possible. Make contact with [Brigadier] General [John H.] Church [the Far East Command's highest-ranking representative in Korea]. If you can't find him, go to Taejon and beyond if you can. Sorry I can't give you more information—that's all I've got. Good luck, and God bless you and your men![31]

Task Force Smith, named after its commander, arrived at an airfield near Pusan on July 1. Woefully tiny, ill-armed, and poorly equipped, it consisted of 440 officers and men, including two under-strength rifle companies (B and C) of the 1st Battalion and half of its headquarters company (clerks, cooks, and other staff people). It also included a two-gun 75-millimeter (three-inch) recoilless rifle platoon from M Company, 3rd Battalion, 21st Regiment, and two 4.2-inch (10.7-centimeter) mortars from the regiment's heavy mortar company. Each man carried 120 rounds of ammunition for his rifle and two days' combat rations, which contained three canned meals. Only about 17 percent of these men had ever faced an enemy and most were 20 years old or younger.

The task force boarded trains in Pusan and rattled into Taejon the next morning, where Smith quickly found General Church. "We have a little action up here," the general told Smith, stabbing at a map. "All we need is some men up there who won't run when they see tanks. We're going to move you up to support the ROKs and give them some moral support."[32]

Smith, leaving his unit behind, then scouted ahead to an area about three miles (five kilometers) north of Osan, a village situated between Seoul and Taejon on the main Seoul-Pusan highway. He found an ideal blocking position along a line of low rolling hills about 300 feet (91 meters) above the level avenue of approach. This commanding position overlooked the main railway line to the east and afforded a clear view to Suwon, some eight miles (13 kilometers) to the north.

The next day, July 3, Major General William F. Dean flew into Taejon to take command of the U.S. 24th Infantry division. Taejon, South Korea's sixth largest city, is located 100 miles (161 kilometers) south of Seoul. Dean planned to make it his command post. Meanwhile, to the north, the NKPA continued to press southward unchecked. Inchon (In'chon), ten miles (16 kilometers) west-southwest of Seoul, fell to the Communists that same day.

Troops from Task Force Smith, 24th Infantry Division, depart for the war front from Taejon railroad station in July 1950.

On July 4, Task Force Smith was joined in Pyongtaek (P'yongt'aek) by part of the 52nd Field Artillery Battalion, comprising six 105-millimeter (four-inch) howitzers, 73 vehicles, and 108 men under the command of Lieutenant Colonel Miller O. Perry. Smith, Perry, and a few others moved forward and confirmed the blocking position that Smith had selected. In the early morning hours of July 5, Smith moved his combined infantry and artillery into position north of Osan. Arriving at 3:00 A.M. in cold, rainy weather, Smith's troops dug foxholes and prepared themselves for their first encounter with the enemy.

Shortly after 7:00 A.M., forward elements of the North Korean 4th Division, supported by the 107th Tank Battalion, 105th Armored Brigade, advanced toward the task force's positions. Smith ordered artillery fire on the enemy armor, but that did not stop the advance of 30 T-34 medium tanks. Nor did direct hits from Smith's 75-millimeter recoilless rifles or 2.36-inch (6-centimeter) antitank rocket launchers hold back the T-34s. (A 3.5-inch [9-centimeter] rocket would have proved effective against the T-34s, but there was none in Korea at that time.) As the tanks approached Perry's artillery positions, one of his 105-millimeter howitzers firing AT (antitank) rounds knocked out two tanks but did not stop the advance of the others. The tanks quickly neutralized the 105-millimeter howitzer and continued unimpeded, followed by the North Korean infantry. "In a little less than two hours, 30 North Korean tanks rolled through the position we were supposed to block as if we hadn't been there," recalled First Lieutenant William Wyrick. "That was our first two hours in combat."[33]

After a brief lull in the action, Smith's positions underwent a second tank-supported infantry attack at 10:00 A.M. Although American fire exacted a heavy toll of NKPA infantry casualties, the T-34s again advanced unimpeded. When Smith attempted to disengage his forces and fall back to a secondary blocking position farther south, heavy enemy fire and much greater numbers sent the poorly trained, armed, and equipped Americans withdrawing in some disarray and occasionally in near-precipitous flight. First Lieutenant Philip Day, Jr., remembered:

> It was raining still, and it was lousy. No one set up another defensive position. We moved as fast as we could. Everything had broken down and it was every man for himself. I was in a small column. We kept to the rice paddies and away from the road where we knew the NK [North Korean] tanks were. If we heard something, we went the other way. All day we wandered around over the landscape.[34]

When the survivors of Task Force Smith reassembled at Taejon several days later, five officers and 148 enlisted men were missing from their ranks and presumed dead, missing, or captured. During the fighting, an anonymous American machine gunner had become the first U.S. battle death of the Korean War. The battle cost the North Koreans 42 dead and 85 wounded. Four NK tanks were either destroyed or immobilized. Tiny Task Force Smith had succeeded in delaying the enemy advance for about seven hours. An entry in a diary taken from a killed North Korean soldier noted: "Near Osan there was a great battle." [35] A monument at Osan still marks the site of that battle.

As U.S. reinforcements poured into South Korea from Japan, the North Koreans continued their southward drive with additional successes against more and more elements of Bill Dean's 24th Division. On July 6, the NKPA forced Dean's 34th Regiment to withdraw from the next blocking position at Pyongtaek after a minimal delay. Two days later, after another short delaying action, his 21st Regiment abandoned Chonan (Ch'onan). Dean later wrote:

> A sweating officer coming from Ch'onan told us that North Korean tanks were in the town, although we could not see them. He said Colonel [Robert B.] Martin had grabbed a bazooka [rocket launcher] and was leading his men with it, actually forcing the tanks to turn and run, when one tank came around the corner unexpectedly and fired from less than 25 feet. The shot blew Colonel Martin in half. Thereafter, resistance had disintegrated and now our troops were bugging out. [36]

In New York the next day, July 7, the UN Security Council asked the United States to act as its executor for the Korean War and to assemble a UN Command (UNC) to fight it. The United States accepted the responsibility and

U.S. machine guns overlook the Kap-ch'on River on the outskirts of Taejon.

President Truman named General MacArthur to head the command on July 8.

Back in Korea, the NKPA pressed relentlessly south-ward, delayed by Dean's 21st Regiment at Chochiwon (Choch'iwon) only until July 12. In the meantime, between July 10 and July 18, General MacArthur rushed the 25th Infantry Division from bases in Japan to South Korea, while the 1st Cavalry Division started loading at Yokohama for imminent movement to the same destination. Events now moved fast.

On July 13, 8th U.S. Army commander Walton H. Walker arrived in Korea to establish EUSA Forward Headquarters at Taegu, where he assumed command of all U.S. ground forces in Korea. Two days later, the 29th Regimental Combat Team embarked for Korea from Okinawa. Then, on July 17, General MacArthur delegated command of all ROK ground forces to General Walker. When other UN forces arrived in Korea, they also passed to Walker's command.

The next day, lead elements of the 1st Cavalry Division landed unopposed at Pohang on the east coast of Korea. General Walker asked Bill Dean's embattled 24th Division to hold the line at Taejon for two days while the 1st Cavalry troops moved into position. The 24th held, but with no time to spare. Taejon fell on July 20. In the muddled haze that shrouded the battle zone, Bill Dean vanished. As the Americans would learn later, Dean had become separated from his unit, injured in a fall, and subsequently taken prisoner after eluding the NKPA for 36 days.

On July 27, General MacArthur flew into Taegu to confer with General Walker. MacArthur expressed grave concerns that any further withdrawals might jeopardize Pusan and even force EUSA to evacuate the peninsula. The supreme commander made it clear to Walker that he wanted no forced evacuation from Korea. Walker got MacArthur's message and promptly relayed it to his 25th Division field commanders:

There will be no Dunkirk [evacuation of British and French troops from the European continent at Dunkirk, France, May 26–June 4, 1940], there will be no Bataan [surrender of U.S.-Filipino defenders of the Bataan Peninsula, Luzon, Philippine Islands, on April 8, 1941], a retreat to Pusan would be one of the greatest butcheries in history. We must fight until the end. Capture by these people is worse than death itself. We will fight as a team. If some of us must die, we will die fighting together. Any man who gives ground may be personally responsible for the death of thousands of his comrades.

I want everybody to understand that we are going to hold this line. We are going to win.[37]

Walker's grim instructions became known as his "stand or die" order. His soldiers stood—and many died.

All the while, reinforcements kept pouring in to Korea. The 5th Regimental Combat Team arrived on the last day of July, followed by lead elements of the 2nd Infantry Division from Fort Lewis, Washington, on August 1, and the 1st Marine Provisional Brigade from

Strategies and Tactics

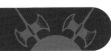

When nations go to war, they use tactics—the art of placing or maneuvering forces skillfully in battle—to accomplish their military or political strategy, a plan or policy for achieving a desired end. Reduced to its simplest terms, the North Korean and Chinese strategy during the Korean War was to reunite the two Koreas as a single Communist nation. Conversely, the strategy of the United Nations called for the preservation of South Korea's independence, and for the containment of the spread of communism in Asia. The tactics of the opposing forces derived largely from the means most available to each side for waging war, which resulted in pitting Communist manpower against UN firepower.

When assaulting UN defensive positions, the Communist armies employed human waves of attackers. They often attempted to overcome superior UN firepower by the sheer weight of their numbers. Attacking in three or four waves, they were willing to accept the huge casualties that their suicidal attacks would inevitably yield. In the early phases of the Korean War, the Communists would send forcibly drafted and untrained South Korean youths in the first wave, progressively better trained forces in the second and third waves, and finally their best troops in the fourth wave. The blare of bugles, the banging of pans, and a variety of horrific screams frequently preceded and accompanied such fanatical attacks.

Despite the frightening aspects of these chilling human-wave attacks, they rarely prevailed against well-disciplined UN troops with superior firepower. Such fanaticism usually succeeded only in demonstrating the Communists' utter disregard for the loss of human life—most of which losses were their own.

Camp Pendleton, California, the next day. On August 4, General Walker established the Naktong Perimeter—better known as the Pusan Perimeter—and the UN forces (chiefly U.S. and ROK units) dug in for a last stand to save the Republic of Korea.

General Walker, seated in the rear of the jeep to the left, established the Naktong, or Pusan, Perimeter with instructions to the soldiers to "stand or die."

The Pusan Perimeter

For five weeks we have been trading space for time. The space is running out for us. The time is running out for our enemies.

—*The New York Times*, July 29, 1950
(quoted in D. Randall Beirne, "Pusan Perimeter," in
The Korean War: An Encyclopedia, edited by Stanley Sandler)

The Pusan Perimeter roughly resembled a vertical rectangle. In the north it ran due west from Yongdok on the east coast for about 50 miles (81 kilometers) through high, rugged mountains; then it turned sharply and ran due south for 80 miles (129 kilometers), mostly along the Naktong River, Korea's second largest. Finally it left the river where the Naktong turns eastward and extended another 20 miles (32 kilometers) south to the seacoast near Masan. Some of the fiercest fighting occurred there, where there was no natural barrier. The remaining two sides were bounded by water, the Korea Strait in the south and the Sea of Japan in the east.

To defend the perimeter, General Walker positioned five ROK divisions in the north—the 1st, 3rd, 6th, 8th, and Capital Divisions. The ROKs were strung through the mountains from the east coast and around the corner to Waegwan, about a third of the way down the western side. Walker covered the rest of the front from Waegwan to the south coast with his three American divisions, the 24th and 25th Infantry and the 1st Cavalry Divisions.

North Korean Premier Kim Il Sung had set August 15, the fifth anniversary of Korea's liberation from Japanese rule, as the date for Korean reunification. By August 4, time was fast running out on Kim's pledge. And Walker's forces had reached the last natural barrier that separated Pusan from Kim's advancing armies. Further, retreat would no longer be an option.

On paper, General Walker's defense perimeter consisted of a continuous line. In the field, it did not. At that time, the U.S. Army's tactical doctrine considered 10,000 yards (9,144 meters), or five miles, to be a practicable operational sector for a division. Along Walker's perimeter, battalions— officially one-ninth of a division—were defending 15,000-yard (13,716-meter) fronts. This produced a string of company- or platoon-sized outposts on hills rather than an unbroken line.

Despite this apparent paucity of forces, however, as later studies would reveal, the UN forces were much better off than either MacArthur or Walker realized at the time. Thirteen North Korean (NK) divisions had suffered heavy losses on their southward drive and would sustain even heavier losses in the ensuing fighting.

By the time the North Korean forces reached the perimeter, Walker's UN defenders actually enjoyed a personnel advantage over the enemy of about 92,000 to 70,000. (Actually, there were some 114,000 UN personnel inside the perimeter, though 22,000 were support troops and half of the combat troops were South Korean.) Despite their numerical disadvantage, the North Koreans still held the initiative, and the UN forces still faced a real possibility of a Dunkirk-style evacuation.

Upon arriving at the perimeter, seven divisions of the NKPA's 1st Corps lined up opposite the U.S. divisions along the Masan front, southwest of the Naktong River line. Above 1st Corps, six divisions of the NKPA's 2nd Corps tied in with it and stretched northwest to face ROK forces at Waegwan and farther north and eastward across the top of the perimeter. Although the situation looked grim to both Walker and MacArthur, their forces now had certain advantages beyond numerical superiority over the enemy that they had not held up till now.

For the first time, Walker's forces had established a near-continuous defense line that afforded them the important advantage of interior lines, which meant shorter supply lines. Distances from the port of Pusan to key points along the perimeter measured 63 miles (101 kilometers) northeast to Pohang, 55 miles (89 kilometers) northwest to Taegu, and 29 miles (47 kilometers) west to Masan. Within 15 miles (24 kilometers) of the port, where supplies and troops were pouring in, Walker had set up numerous depots and dumps from which men and materiel could be easily rushed to the front. Moreover, UN air and naval forces controlled the air and waters around the peninsula. In short, Walker's troops were well fed, equipped, reinforced, and supported.

By contrast, the North Koreans had extended their supply lines to the maximum, from the 38th parallel to the tip of the Korean Peninsula. Aircraft of the U.S. 5th Air Force, Navy, and Marines restricted enemy supply movements to the hours of darkness, and even then to a painfully slow pace on the backs of humans and animals. By the time the North Korean armies reached the Pusan Perimeter, they had lost some 58,000 troops. Most of their remaining 70,000 men—including many South Koreans who had been forcibly enlisted into their ranks—were exhausted, half-starved, and critically short of ammunition, clothing, and medical supplies. They lacked air and naval support, and the UN forces had reduced NKPA armor to about 40 tanks by August 4.

Yet, in their zeal to drive the UN forces into the sea before August 15, the North Koreans continued to advance toward Pusan, sacrificing wave upon wave of troops to superior UN firepower. On July 28, the NK 6th Infantry Division, the conquerors of Seoul, took up positions to the west of the perimeter, near Chinju and Masan. Division commander Major General Wae Pang told his troops, "The task given to us is . . . the annihilation of the remnants of the enemy. . . . [T]he liberation of Chinju and Masan means the final battle to cut off the windpipe of the enemy. . . . Men of the 6th Division, let us annihilate the enemy and distinguish ourselves."[38]

During the next five days, while Pang prepared his division for the attack, the U.S. 5th Regimental Combat Team (RCT) and the 1st Provisional Marine Brigade arrived in Korea from Schofield Barracks, Hawaii, and Camp Pendleton, California, respectively. General Walker merged the two newly arrived units with the 24th and 35th Infantry Regiments of Major General William B. Kean's 25th Infantry Division to form Task Force Kean. Walker, heartened by the new arrivals—and perhaps prematurely optimistic—decided to use the new task force in a limited offensive in the Masan sector.

Troops of the provisional brigade were the first marines to reach Korea. Their no-nonsense commander, Brigadier General Edward A. Craig, who had earned the Navy Cross on Guam during World War II, told his commanders that their brigade would be used as shock troops. "The Pusan Perimeter is like a weakened dike, and we will be used to plug holes in it as they open," he said. "It will be costly fighting against a numerically superior enemy." He paused briefly, then continued quietly, "Gentlemen, Marines have never lost a battle. This Brigade will not be the first to establish such a precedent."[39] On August 7, the eighth anniversary of the 5th Marines' historic landing at Guadalcanal during World War II, Craig's marines joined the battle in Korea, eager to keep their traditions intact.

The marine brigade advanced westward from Masan toward Sachon, on the left flank of Task Force Kean's three-pronged attack to capture Chinju and Sachon (Sach'on). General Kean assigned the 35th Regiment on the right and the 5th RCT in the middle to capture Chinju; the marines, Sachon. He held the 24th Regiment in reserve. After eliminating the NK 6th Division and securing Chinju and Sachon, Walker planned for the task force to swing north to the Kum River and envelop the NK 4th Division in front of Major General John H. Church's 24th Infantry Division. (Church had assumed command of the 24th Division for its missing commander, William F. Dean, on July 22.) While Walker's forces moved to the west, Wae Pang's 6th Division commenced its eastward drive toward Masan.

Task Force Kean got off to a good start in the north. The 35th Regiment overran a key North Korean position called "the Notch," a pass on the northern Chinju-Masan road southwest of Chungam-ni. After a five-hour battle, the 35th Regiment advanced rapidly toward Muchon-ni.

It was during the Korean War that helicopters were first used at the front for evacuating wounded troops and delivering vital communications.

In the task force's central sector, however, the 5th RCT took a wrong turn onto the road assigned to the marines, and its advance stalled in a road jam at Hill 255 on the Masan Road before it could start.

Soon afterward, the 2nd Battalion, 5th RCT, found itself surrounded by elements of the NK 6th Division on a nearby elevation known as Hill 342. Marine Corps historians Lynn Montross and Nicholas A. Canzona describe it as "a huge molar whose roots rise from the MSR [main supply route] west of Chindong-ni."[40] The task of clearing the blocked road and of extricating their army counterparts from Hill 342 fell to the marines.

Lieutenant Colonel Robert D. Taplett's 3rd Battalion, 5th Marines, was the first marine unit to reach the road jam near Tosan. The battalion surgeon, Navy Lieutenant Robert Harvey, likened the tall, lean Taplett to a race-horse: "What an enlistment poster he'd have made! He spoke in a staccato way with no warmth and seemed hard as nails."[41] Taplett, a 32-year-old native of South Dakota, promptly sent a reinforced platoon to help ward off the NK attackers on Hill 342.

Enemy artillery and NK infiltrators working behind UN lines complicated the task of the marines, but the heat of the Korean summer claimed more marine casualties than the enemy did. The blistering heat, at times in excess of 110°F (43°C), tested the stamina and will of the marines as they struggled toward the top of Hill 342. "Stumbling, gasping for breath, soaked with perspiration," write Montross and Canzona, "every marine reached the point at which he barely managed to drag himself up the steep incline. There were choked curses as men gained a few feet, only to slip and fall back even farther."[42]

The marines and their army brethren engaged soldiers of the NK 6th Division in chaotic, back-and-forth fighting for the next two days and found the North Koreans to be formidable and fierce adversaries. Then, gradually, the men of Task Force Kean gained confidence and momentum and shoved the enemy backward. From August 9 to August 12, the marine brigade—aided by close air support from marine Corsair fighter-bombers off the U.S. light carrier *Badoeng Strait*—drove 26 miles (42 kilometers) in four days and expected to reach Sachon the next day. But before the marines could capture their objective, General Kean, with the NK 6th Army's drive halted, recalled his task force to meet a new threat.

At his headquarters, Kean assigned a new task to General Craig's marines, now known as a "fire brigade" (for their ability to move rapidly to hot spots and put out fires). Craig later wrote, "Kean informed me that two Communist divisions had broken through the Naktong area and it would be necessary for the brigade to pull out from the drive and move to the Naktong, where it was to restore that position to its original status."[43]

The North Korean 4th Army posed the major threat at the so-called Naktong Bulge—a westward loop in the river that forms an area four by five miles (six by eight kilometers), about a third of the way up the perimeter. East of the bulge lay the Miryang railhead, whose capture would cut the main supply route from Pusan to Taegu and force Walker to withdraw his forces into a virtually indefensible slaughter pen. General Church's 24th Infantry Division stood between the North Koreans, who had started crossing the river on August 6, and potential disaster.

The marines joined Church's division at Miryang on August 15. A British military observer watched the now battle-hardened marines pass through Miryang on the way to the First Battle of the Naktong Bulge and wrote:

> If Miryang is lost Taegu becomes untenable and we will be faced with a withdrawal from Korea. I am heartened that the Marine Brigade will move against the Naktong salient [bulge] tomorrow. . . . these Marines have the swagger, confidence and hardness that must have been in Stonewall Jackson's army of the Shenandoah. . . . Upon this thin line of reasoning. I cling to the hope of victory.[44]

That same day, Task Force Hill—roughly three army regiments under Colonel John G. Hill, U.S. Army—had failed to halt the advancing NK 4th Army. General Walker rushed to General Church's headquarters and said, "I am going to give you the Marine brigade. I want this situation cleaned up, and quick."[45] To repair the situation and shove the North Koreans back across the Naktong, the marines first had to drive them off Obong-ni Ridge and out of its hilly and swampy surrounds.

Lynn Montross described Obong-ni Ridge, soon dubbed No-Name Ridge by the marines, as resembling "some huge prehistoric reptile,"[46] with its head overlooking Tugok and its long body sprawling southeast for a mile and a half. This giant serpent was to become the site of the marines' bloodiest battle of the peninsula war. Lieutenant Colonel Harold S. Roise's 2nd Battalion, 5th Marines, jumped off against the ridge at 8:00 A.M. on August 17. *Time* magazine correspondent James Bell watched the marines move up the hill and wrote:

> Hell burst around the leathernecks [marines] as they moved up the barren face of the ridge. Everywhere along the assault line, men dropped. To continue looked impossible. But, all glory forever to the bravest men I ever saw, the line did not break. The casualties were unthinkable, but the assault force never turned back. It moved, fell down, got up and moved again.[47]

Brigade commander Craig, who was also observing the assault through binoculars from a roadway in the valley, echoed the correspondent's words. "I never saw men with so much guts," he said.[48] But guts did not get the job done that morning.

Sixty percent of Roise's battalion went down before noon, and the attack failed. Lieutenant Colonel Raymond L. Murray, regimental commander of the 5th Marines and holder of the Navy Cross for his actions on Saipan in World War II, later reported, "2/5 took a terrible beating."[49] Walker added two more army regiments to the fray—the 9th and 19th Infantry Regiments. The marines and soldiers fought back desperately.

The North Koreans struck the marine positions with four Soviet-built T-34 tanks. The marines countered with Corsairs and their own M26 Pershing medium tanks, while the marine infantrymen cut loose at the T-34s with 75-millimeter recoilless rifles and 3.5-inch rocket launchers. In five minutes, the marines smashed all four seemingly invincible T-34s and turned them into flaming coffins.

The furious fighting continued far into the night, with no holds barred. Lieutenant Colonel Joseph H. Alexander, a retired marine, combat veteran, and military historian, described the ensuing action:

> On the heels of a punishing mortar attack, NKPA infantry blew bugles, fired flares, and swarmed against the Marine positions. Hand-to-hand fighting erupted in a dozen places. Marine positions were overrun, recaptured, lost again. Sergeants succeeded fallen lieutenants, patched together makeshift platoons, counterattacked again. And again.[50]

The next day, marine Corsairs came back on station, and Taplett's 3rd Battalion swept the hills to the west. By mid-afternoon of the second day, the marines held No-Name Ridge, and the remnants of the NK 4th Division were fleeing west across the river. On August 19, army and marine forces met at the river, and the First Battle of the

U.S. infantrymen in Korea cover their ears as a 75-millimeter recoilless rifle is fired at the front lines.

Naktong Bulge ended. The victory cost the marines some 350 casualties, but they had destroyed more than 4,000 of their enemy. After the battle, the 24th Division buried more than 1,200 enemy dead.

Meanwhile, during the middle two weeks of August, the North Koreans launched a major offensive north of Taegu, spearheaded by the NK 3rd Division. Arrayed against them stood Lieutenant General Paik Sun Yup's 7,000-man ROK 1st Division, without tanks or howitzers for support. By August 12, the North Koreans had driven to within 12 miles (19 kilometers) of Taegu. South Korean President Syngman Rhee moved his capital to Pusan, and General Paik issued a command similar to General Walker's "stand or die" order. "This will be our final defense line," he told his troops, emphasizing that "the fate of the nation rests squarely on the backs of the ROK 1st Division."[51]

Paik's overmatched ROKs fought a valiant blocking action on three fronts but could not hold without help. General Walker sent emergency reinforcements from the ROK 10th Division. He also ordered Lieutenant Colonel John H. "Iron Mike" Michaelis's crack 27th "Wolfhound" Regiment of the 25th Division, along with Colonel Paul L. Freeman, Jr.'s 23rd Regiment of the recently arrived 2nd Infantry Division, to join the battle. The American forces deployed on a defensive line in the Tabu-dong corridor, 13 miles (21 kilometers) northwest of Taegu, while the ROKs occupied the hills on either side of it. The narrow corridor represented the gateway to Taegu and Pusan. American soldiers soon dubbed the battleground the "Bowling Alley" because of the look and sound occasioned by a booming encounter down a two-and-a-half-mile-long road bracketed by mountains.

Beginning on the night of August 18 and continuing through August 27, the North Koreans poured into the corridor with tanks and infantry and drove southward. The NK tanks opened fire on the Americans. Red balls of cannon fire whooshed down the narrow chute and exploded. Echoes of shell fire bounced off the bracketing hills like bowling pins rattling off a wall. Under the eerie light of flares, American rocket launchers, tanks, and artillery destroyed the NK tanks and turned back the attackers with heavy losses. The

NK 3rd Division ceased to exist. Even so, each night brought more of the same.

On August 20, an ROK unit pulled back under heavy attack, leaving the left flank of Iron Mike's Wolfhounds exposed. Hoping to avoid a "bug out," a panicky retreat, Michaelis told the battalion commander on his threatened flank: "If we lose this battle, we may not have a Korea. We have nowhere else to go. We must stand and fight."[52] And they did, along with General Paik's heroic 1st Division.

When the Battle of the Bowling Alley ended on August 27, the UN forces had ripped the NK 1st and 13th Divisions and regained all lost positions on their last line of defense. Paik's valiant ROKs had lost 2,300 killed and wounded. In return, however, they had killed 5,700 invaders. With the threat to the Tabu-dong corridor stabilized, the Americans left to join the fighting farther south.

Meanwhile, in mid-August, the U.S. 1st Cavalry Division met and stopped an assault by the NK 10th Division along a 35-mile (56-kilometer) front south of Waegwan. On August 17, soldiers of the 5th Cavalry Regiment recaptured Hill 303 near Waegwan and found the bodies of 26 U.S. soldiers who had been bound and raked with burp-gun (submachine gun) bullets. Roy E. Appleman, an official army historian, described the NK atrocity:

> The boys lay packed tightly, shoulder to shoulder, lying on their sides, curled like babies sleeping in the sun. Their feet, bloodied and bare, from walking on rocks, stuck out stiffly. . . . All had hands tied behind their backs, some with cord, others with regular issue army communication wire. Only a few of the hands were clenched.[53]

Such atrocities by the North Koreans were by no means

A South Korean soldier comforts a wounded friend before he is evacuated for medical treatment.

uncommon, but the UN forces made the Communists pay for their barbarism.

By the end of August, U.S. and ROK soldiers had severely shattered the NK 1st, 3rd, 10th, and 13th Divisions, and NK casualties in the central sector of the perimeter alone totaled almost 10,000. While the fighting raged around Taegu, the ROK 3rd, 8th, and Capital Divisions battled furiously against the NK 5th and 12th Divisions. From August 10 through August 20, the ROKs lost and recaptured the port of Pohang in the northeast corner of the perimeter. The ROKs all but destroyed the NK 12th Division and killed 3,800 men.

Despite the continuing drain on NKPA numbers, and the accelerated influx of UN reinforcements—including the 27th British Brigade—the North Koreans were not done yet. In late August, the NKPA, now led by General Kim Chaik and reconstituted to a force of some 98,000 men, launched the Great Naktong Offensive, which would last until September 15. Kim's army struck all along the perimeter in a last desperate effort to push through to Pusan. Some of the fiercest fighting again erupted in the Naktong Bulge. Again General Walker called upon General Craig's fire brigade.

The 5th Marines rushed to the bulge—this time to serve with the U.S. 2nd Infantry Division, their old World War I division—griping all the while in typical marine fashion about having to take Obong-ni Ridge all over again. This time, though, soldiers of the NK 9th Division were well supported by T-34 tanks and swarmed out of the hills to take on the marines.

A driving rain canceled marine air support, but marine tanks and infantry antitank weapons, coupled with army and marine artillery and mortar fire, blasted the NK tanks apart and left them burning on the battlefield. The Second Battle of the Naktong Bulge (September 3–5) ended when the North Koreans fled back across the Naktong after three days of savage fighting.

At this point, though fighting continued to rage all along the Pusan Perimeter, General of the Army Douglas

Police Matters

A t the outset of the Korean War, Senator William F. Knowland of California spoke on the floor of the U.S. Senate and said, "The action this government is taking [in Korea] is a police action against a violator of the law of nations and the charter of the United Nations."[*] During a news conference on June 27, 1950, a reporter asked President Harry Truman whether he agreed with the senator's characterization of the Korean incident as a police action under the United Nations. Truman answered, "Yes, that is exactly what it amounts to."[**] Although Truman did not coin the phrase "police action," it has ever since been associated with him. Upon hearing of Truman's statement, some U.S. combat troops in Korea painted the sides of their tanks and landing craft with the motto "Harry's Police."

A few weeks later, the president embroiled himself in another "police matter." As a former artillery officer in the army during World War I, Truman felt that the marines were receiving more than their proper share of acclaim for their actions in Korea. In response to a congressman's suggestion that the marine commandant be given a voice among the Joint Chiefs of Staff, Truman lashed out against the sea soldiers. "For your information," he replied, "the Marine Corps is the Navy's police force and as long as I am president that is what it will remain. They have a propaganda machine that is almost equal to Stalin's."[***]

When Truman's letter appeared in the press on September 5, just ten days before the marines landed at Inchon, it evoked a firestorm of public outrage. Truman apologized publicly to Marine Commandant Clifton B. Cates. After the marines' phenomenal success at Inchon, the president kept any further opinions of them to himself.

[*] Quoted in Robert J. Dvorchak, and the writers and photographers of the Associated Press, *Battle for Korea: The Associated Press History of the Korean Conflict.* Conshohocken, PA: Combined Books, 1993, p. 13.

[**] Ibid., p. 14.

[***] Quoted in Joseph H. Alexander, with Don Horan and Norman C. Stahl, *A Fellowship of Valor: The Battle History of the United States Marines.* New York: HarperCollins, 1997, p. 271.

MacArthur ordered General Walker to pull the marines off line. In a single month of fighting, General Craig's 1st Provisional Marine Brigade had launched four counter-attacks and killed or wounded more than 10,000 North Koreans. Marine casualties totaled about 900, a favorable ratio of better than ten to one. Now MacArthur had them earmarked to play the major role in one of the boldest military counterstrokes ever imagined and successfully executed—the invasion of Inchon.

Generals Whitney, Almond, and MacArthur (commander-in-chief of UN forces) observe the shelling of the port city of Inchon from their post aboard the U.S.S. *Mount McKinley.*

Inchon

The essence of the [Inchon] operation depended upon a great amphibious movement, but the chairman of the Joint Chiefs of Staff, General Omar Bradley, was of the considered opinion that such amphibious operations were obsolete—that there would never be another successful movement of this sort.

—General of the Army Douglas MacArthur (in *Reminiscences*)

General MacArthur, supreme commander of UN forces in Korea, began preparing his brilliant counterstroke against the NPKA shortly after his first visit to the battlefront. On June 29, 1950, from the banks of the Han River, just four days after the NKPA had crossed the 38th parallel into

South Korea, MacArthur observed the "complete and disorganized flight" of the South Korean forces, and the "writhing, dust-shrouded mass"[54] of refugees plodding south, just in front of the advancing invaders. "I watched for an hour the pitiful evidence of the disaster I had inherited," he wrote later. "In that brief interval on the blood-soaked hill I formulated my plans."[55] His plans called for an amphibious landing behind enemy lines at a place called Inchon.

The seaport city of Inchon lies not quite halfway up the west coast of the Korean Peninsula on the Yellow Sea. Inchon services the South Korean capital of Seoul, 20 miles (32 kilometers) to the east. During his initial evaluation of the battle scene, MacArthur recognized at once that Seoul held the key to victory. Not only did it have enormous symbolic and political significance, but strategically it also served as the hub for the only double-tracked railway in Korea and the only surfaced roads sufficient for supplying the North Korean invaders as they moved farther and farther south. Since a few north-south dirt roads farther inland were inadequate for use as supply routes, MacArthur further recognized that a landing at Inchon and the recapture of Seoul would enable his forces to sever the NKPA's supply lines. No army can survive for long without food, oil, and ammunition—particularly when forced to fight on two fronts. Armed with a vision, MacArthur set out to implement it upon his return to Tokyo.

One morning early in July 1950, Lieutenant General Lemuel C. Shepherd, Jr., visited General MacArthur in his office in the Dai-ichi Building in Tokyo. Shepherd was commander of the Fleet Marine Force (FMF), Pacific—the Marine Corps' amphibious force in readiness. MacArthur pointed to his wall map and said to his visitor, "Lem, if I had that First Marine Division, I'd land it here at Inchon."[56] He wanted to know whether Shepherd could deliver the division to Korea, fully equipped and combat ready, by September 15.

Shepherd, who had served under MacArthur in the Pacific during World War II, thought about the proposal. At the time, the 1st Provisional Marine Brigade—which had been formed mostly from units of the 1st Marine Division at Camp Pendleton, California—was already en route to Korea. To reform the division, ship it to Korea, and reunite it with the provisional brigade would take time, and MacArthur wanted it on line in 67 days. Shepherd, eager for a piece of the action for his marines, said, "General, why don't you ask for them?"[57] MacArthur did, the Marine Corps delivered the division, and plans for "Operation Chromite"—the UN code name for the Inchon landing—moved forward.

Initially, MacArthur's choice of a landing site met strong resistance from the Joint Chiefs of Staff (JCS) in Washington, D.C. The JCS felt that the shallowness of the entire Yellow Sea, and that extreme tidal differences that ranged from 23 feet to 35 feet (7 to 11 meters) at Inchon posed too great a danger for ships and landing craft. Low tide transformed the entire inner harbor into a vast mud flat that would strand even the smallest landing craft. Furthermore, the islands of Wolmi-do and Sowolmi-do, linked together by a causeway, formed a strong obstacle that would need softening up by an air and naval bombardment before the actual invasion commenced, thus forfeiting any chance for surprise. The Joint Chiefs also opposed the idea of pulling the marine brigade off the Pusan Perimeter to fill out the 1st Marine Division, thereby weakening Walker's defenses.

On August 23, in a meeting in Tokyo, MacArthur formally proposed his plan to Army Chief of Staff

General J. Lawton Collins and Chief of Naval Operations Admiral Forrest P. Sherman and several other high-level officers. The JCS suggested Kunsan, a small port about 100 miles (161 kilometers) south of Inchon and some 70 air miles (113 kilometers) west of the Pusan defense line, as an alternate landing site. MacArthur rejected Kunsan as being too far south: "Better no flank movement than one such as this."[58] He similarly disdained a second JCS alternative to break out of the perimeter with General Walker's 8th Army. "The enemy will merely roll back on his lines of supply and communication," he said.[59]

After listening patiently to the arguments against his proposal, MacArthur took the floor for a 45-minute oratory in support of his plan. He delivered his arguments with his characteristically dramatic flair, stating, in part, that the

> seizure of Inchon and Seoul will cut the enemy's supply line and seal off the entire southern peninsula. . . . By seizing Seoul I would completely paralyze the enemy's supply system—coming and going. This in turn will paralyze the fighting power of the troops that now face Walker. Without munitions and food they will soon be helpless and disorganized, and can easily be overpowered by our smaller but well-supplied forces.[60]

MacArthur paused frequently for dramatic effect. Methodically, he pointed out that the only alternative to his idea was the continuation of the slaughter of Walker's forces along the defensive perimeter. He also argued that the prestige of the Western world hung in the balance, that a loss to communism in Asia would gravely jeopardize the fate of Europe, and that a victory in Korea would ensure Europe's continued freedom. "Make the wrong decision here—the fatal decision of inertia—and we will be done," he told his audience. "I can almost hear the ticking of the second hand of destiny. We must act now or we will die."[61] After a final pause, he concluded with an assurance of success:

> If my estimate is inaccurate and should I run into a defense with which I cannot cope, I will be there personally and will immediately withdraw our forces before they are committed in a bloody setback. The only loss then will be my professional reputation. But Inchon will not fail. Inchon will succeed. And it will save 100,000 lives.[62]

On August 29, MacArthur received a telegram from the Joint Chiefs in Washington: "We concur after reviewing the information brought back by General Collins and Admiral Sherman, in making preparations and executing a turning movement by amphibious forces on the west coast of Korea—at Inchon."[63] Operation Chromite was on!

Once the JCS had given the go-ahead, the selection, organization, and assembly of the right personnel for the landing followed. On August 26, anticipating the approval of his plan, MacArthur had already activated 10th Corps Headquarters (HQ) in Tokyo. He formed it around his existing General Headquarters Far East Command, under Major General Edward M. "Ned" Almond, his chief of staff. Almond also retained his staff position. By September 15, or D day (the target date for the landing), the 10th Corps would basically consist of two maneuver divisions: the 1st Marine Division, the assault force, commanded by Major General Oliver P. Smith; and the 7th Infantry Division, the sole remaining army division in Japan, led by Major General David G. Barr.

Upon embarkation for Inchon, the 1st Marine Division—with the 1st and 5th Regiments and attachments, including 2,760 army troops and 2,786 Korean marines, and joined later by the reconstituted 7th Marine Regiment—would number 25,040. The 7th Infantry Division contained the 17th, 31st, and 32nd Infantry Regiments. With attachments, including 8,600 ill-trained Korean recruits assigned to it, the division would total 24,815 men. Additional support units (beyond those contained in each division) would include the 56th Amphibious Tank and Tractor Battalion; the 92nd and 96th Field Artillery Battalions (155-millimeter (six-inch) howitzers); the 50th Antiaircraft Artillery Battalion; the 9th Engineer Combat Group; the 2nd Engineer Special Brigade; and others. In total, the 10th Corps invasion force would number approximately 70,000 men on D day.

Command of the invasion fleet, identified as Joint Task Force Seven, and responsibility for the amphibious phase of the operation fell to Vice Admiral Arthur D. Struble, commander of the U.S. 7th Fleet. Struble, a veteran expeditionary force commander, named Rear Admiral James H. Doyle, MacArthur's amphibious operations specialist, as his second-in-command. Struble would command an invasion fleet of more than 230 ships; Doyle would direct the actual landings.

On September 4—while the invasion personnel assembled in haste from as far away as the United States, Great Britain, and Australia—MacArthur completed his invasion plan. He selected September 15 as D day because the tides would rise to their highest point on that date, with the morning tide at 6:59 A.M. and the evening tide at 5:30 P.M. In accord with these high tides, MacArthur and his war planners scheduled a battalion landing team of the 5th Marines to land at Green Beach, a color-designated beach on Wolmi-do, at 6:30 A.M. They assigned the main landings for 5:30 P.M., with the 1st and 2nd Battalions, 5th Marines landing at Red Beach on Inchon's sea front, while all three battalions of the 1st Marines landed simultaneously at Blue Beach, three miles (five kilometers) to the southeast.

The collective task of the marines was, first, to neutralize NK defenses on Wolmi-do to eliminate any potential crossfire from the island; next, to move inland and seize control of the rail and road lines out of Seoul; then, to secure nearby Kimpo airfield for use by UN aircraft; and, finally, to recapture Seoul itself. The 7th Division was to follow the marines ashore and aid in the recapture of Seoul. Afterward, it would turn to the south and attempt to link up with Walker's newly reinforced 8th Army, which, if all went well, would simultaneously break out of the Pusan Perimeter and advance northward. MacArthur hoped to crush the remnants of the NKPA between his two forces.

On September 8, despite their continued misgivings over MacArthur's plan and choice of a landing site, the Joint Chiefs sent their final endorsement of the operation to President Truman. General of the Army Omar N. Bradley, chairman of the JCS, later noted that their approval remained grudging to the last. "It was really too late in the game for the JCS to formally disapprove Inchon," he wrote.[64]

The world's last great amphibious operation actually commenced five days before D day with air and naval bombardments of Wolmi-do. On September 13, two days before D day, Rear Admiral J.M. Higgins led two U.S. heavy cruisers, two British light cruisers, and six U.S. destroyers up the narrow Flying Fish Channel and opened fire on 75-millimeter gun emplacements on Wolmi-do. Five destroyers anchored off the island and drew fire from the 75-millimeter guns. Naval gunfire and subsequent bombings silenced the enemy guns. A U.S. Navy reconnaissance team led by Lieutenant Eugene F. Clark had discovered the presence of the guns earlier that month. In the early darkness of D day, Clark would also guide the invasion fleet up the channel with a captured navigational beam on Palmi-do, a tiny islet outward of Wolmi-do.

The invasion fleet—more than 230 vessels from the United States, Australia, Canada, New Zealand, France, the Netherlands, and Great Britain—reached the Inchon Narrows just before dawn on September 15. The armada included the cruiser *Rochester*, Admiral Struble's flagship, and the *Mount McKinley*, Admiral Doyle's amphibious command ship, with General MacArthur aboard. Forty-seven LSTs (landing ship, tank) carrying many of the troops and much of their equipment formed the core of Doyle's command.

At 5:08 A.M., the *Mount McKinley* hoisted the U.S. Navy's traditionally terse signal: "Land the landing force."[65] Marines scrambled from their transports into their LCVPs (landing craft, vehicles, personnel) and the invasion of Inchon was under way.

Lieutenant Robert Taplett's 3rd Battalion, 5th Marines, splashed ashore on Wolmi-do at 6:33 A.M. Ignoring scattered enemy gunfire, the marines streamed inland and raised the American flag over Radio Hill, the island's highest point, within 22 minutes. Forty-seven minutes after the marines had landed, Taplett radioed the fleet: "WOLMI-DO SECURED."[66]

Aboard the *Mount McKinley*, MacArthur, upon seeing the flag fluttering over Wolmi-do, put down his binoculars, rose from his swivel chair, and said, "That's it, let's get some coffee."[67] The general's great gamble had paid off. Over coffee, MacArthur wrote a note to send to Admiral

The invasion of Inchon, located halfway up the Korean Peninsula, was MacArthur's finest hour.

Struble: "The Navy and the Marines have never shone more brightly than this morning."[68]

Taplett's battalion had taken its first objective at a cost of 20 wounded marines. In return, Taplett's assault troopers had killed 108 North Koreans, captured 136, and sealed about 100 others who refused to surrender in caves with tank dozers. The day had only just begun, however. Now, the long wait began for the marines on Wolmi-do, who were isolated until the next high tide.

If Taplett's marines experienced any uneasiness in their isolation, the marine Corsairs and navy Skyraiders (attack bombers) circling overhead all morning helped ease their anxieties. Then, at 2:30 P.M., UN warships— cruisers, destroyers, and rocket ships—commenced an offshore naval bombardment that extended some 25 miles (40 kilometers) behind Inchon, blocking the possibility of any major enemy reinforcements from reaching the city.

At 3:30 P.M., two battalions of Lieutenant Colonel Ray Murray's 5th Marines and Colonel Lewis B. "Chesty" Puller's entire 1st Marine Regiment began clambering over the sides of their transports and down cargo nets into their landing craft. A flotilla of LCVPs and LVTs (landing vehicle, tracked) circled about and formed lines of departure. At 4:45 P.M., the bobbing boats crossed the lines and churned toward shore. Precisely according to plan, the 1st Marines landed at Blue Beach, southeast of Wolmi-do, at 5:32 P.M. A minute later, the 5th Marines stormed ashore at Red Beach, northeast of the island. Once ashore, Murray's 5th Marines were to reunite with Taplett's battalion on Wolmi-do and attack eastward through Inchon, while Puller's regiment drove inland to cut the highway to Seoul.

Red Beach actually consisted of a 1,000-foot-long seawall that rose in places to a height of 15 feet. The marines came prepared with ladders to scale the wall. Platoon leader First Lieutenant Baldomero Lopez, of A Company, a 25-year-old regular officer from Tampa, Florida, was one of the first marines over the seawall. He led his third platoon forward. Together, Lopez and his men killed a dozen North Koreans and took out an NK bunker. But a second bunker remained. Second

Lieutenant Tom Gibson of Mortar Company, 5th Marines described the action:

> Lopez began to attack it. Before he could throw the grenade he held in his hand he was hit. The grenade dropped to his side. To save the men of his platoon he rolled over on top of it. Punchy [Lopez] won the Medal of Honor [posthumously] right there on the beach. On the dock at Pusan, he couldn't wait to get at the bastards.[69]

Hundreds of Murray's 5th Marines followed his first wave of attackers, scaling the seawall or pouring through gaping holes blasted in it by naval gunfire. Caught up momentarily in a nasty firefight, the marines advanced relentlessly by fire and maneuver. A report later noted:

> "A" Company, with the mission of taking battalion objective No. 1 (Cemetery Hill) . . . landed amid heavy small arms fire and intermittent mortar fire coming from trenches and bunkers on the beach, from the exposed left flank, and from Cemetery Hill.[70]

The NK defenders quickly broke and ran, and the marines pressed on into the streets of Inchon. Within 20 minutes of the marine assault on Red Beach, a flare rocketed into the sky, signaling the capture Cemetery Hill, the highest point in Inchon.

At the same time, about three miles to the southeast, Chesty Puller's 1st Marines battled their way ashore at Blue Beach, scaling the seawall with ladders, or blasting their way through with dynamite. Smoke and the gathering darkness led to confusion. One group of marines landed to the left of the beach and had to wade ashore. At one point, Admiral Struble's barge approached

Marines patrol near Inchon after Operation Chromite. The daring assault deep into enemy territory cut off North Korean forces farther south.

the seawall and a marine sergeant bellowed: "Boat there! Get the hell out of here!"[71] The combat-wise admiral quietly advised his helmsman to move back into the stream. A minute later, a great explosion ripped the wall apart.

By midnight, the 5th Marines had pushed aside sporadic resistance in the city and penetrated to the top of Observatory Hill. Shortly thereafter, Lieutenant Colonel Allan Sutter's 2nd Battalion, 1st Marines, reached the Inchon-Seoul highway about a mile inland. By 1:30 A.M.

on September 16, the two regiments had encircled the city and secured their first day's objectives. In so doing, the marines sustained 196 casualties: 22 dead and 174 wounded. Of their island landings in the Pacific War, only Guadalcanal and Okinawa had cost fewer men.

Before Inchon, Chairman Omar Bradley of the Joint Chiefs had declared that there would never be another great amphibious movement. MacArthur and his marines proved Bradley wrong. Fleet Admiral William F. "Bull" Halsey hailed the Inchon operation as "the most masterly and audacious strategic stroke in all history."[72] Halsey was not one to award credit lightly.

Not everyone would agree with Halsey's assessment. At the very least, however, the Inchon invasion represents the crowning achievement of General MacArthur's long and distinguished army career, and an illustrious milestone in the fighting history of the U.S. Marines. But for both MacArthur and the Marines, the going was about to grow tougher.

Seoul

The push east toward Seoul after the Inchon invasion proved to be a bloody and arduous action. MacArthur's wish to reach the capital city by September 25 seemed impossible.

I remember one day during "Almond's mopping up" when our battalion gained exactly 1,200 yards. At each barricade we had to annihilate the enemy, evacuate casualties, and wearily go on to the next.

—Staff Sergeant Lee Bergee, E Company, 2nd Battalion, 1st Marines
(quoted in Donald Knox, *The Korean War: Pusan to Chosin*)

At dawn on September 16, 1950, marine commander General O.P. Smith ordered a regiment of ROK marines to clear out the bypassed areas of resistance in Inchon and sent Ray Murray's 5th Marines and Chesty Puller's 1st Marines eastward toward Seoul. The 10th Corps plan now called for the 5th Marines

81

(later reinforced by Colonel Homer L. Litzenberg's hastily formed and late-arriving 7th Marines) to advance through Kimpo, cross the Han River, and move against Seoul from the west. At the same time, the 1st Marines were to secure Yongdung-p'o, an industrial suburb on the south bank of the Han opposite Seoul, and proceed northeast across the river into Seoul. In military parlance, the 5th Marines would operate as the "maneuver" element and rotate about the solid "holding" element, or "hub," provided by the 1st Marines.

While the ROK marines—enraged by reports of NK atrocities against their relatives—went to work clearing out Inchon with ruthless efficiency, the 5th and 1st Marines linked up at the Inchon-Seoul Highway, three miles east of the city, and struck out for their respective objectives at Kimpo and Yongdung-p'o. Murray's regiment immediately ran into six NKPA T-34 tanks. Marine Pershing tanks, 75-mm recoilless rifles, and 3.5-inch rockets cut loose with a series of blinding flashes and took out the T-34s within minutes, while marine riflemen cut down NK infantrymen by the score. "All six of those tanks were burning and there were dead North Koreans lying all over the place," Private First Class Doug Koch of Dog Company recalled later. "That was quite a sight."[73]

As chance would have it, a convoy carrying MacArthur and a group of top-level commanders and reporters arrived at the scene of the recent tank battle. MacArthur got out of his jeep and poked the body of a dead North Korean with his toe. "That's the way I like to see them!" he said. "A good sight for my old eyes!"[74] The architect of Inchon was basking in his glory—but he was also pushing his luck. Shortly after the convoy departed, the marines flushed several armed NK soldiers out of a culvert under the road where MacArthur's jeep had been parked. Koch, an interested onlooker, could not help thinking, "Just think how famous one of them would have been if he'd lobbed a hand grenade onto the road a few minutes before."[75]

MacArthur never worried about such possibilities. Marine General Lem Shepherd, concerned for MacArthur's safety, advised him not to expose himself unnecessarily. "No," MacArthur answered, "anywhere my men are I will go."[76] He did so daily.

Elsewhere, in Yongdung-p'o, the Seoul suburb, Puller's regiment met strong resistance. "Yongdungp'o [sic] was surrounded by a moat on one side, by a wide rice paddy on the west, and by high ridges on the southeast," Staff Sergeant Lee Bergee of E Company recalled later. "Staring at the sooty chimneys of the city, I wondered how many of us would be killed taking this dirty town."[77] Bergee survived the assault on Yongdung-p'o, but many of his comrades did not. It took the 1st Marines three days of heavy fighting to take the "dirty town." Casualties ran high.

Meanwhile, about 180 air miles (290 kilometers) to the south, General Walker's 8th Army began its planned counter-offensive or "breakout" from the Pusan Perimeter on the same day, September 16. Walker directed his attack along three lines: The 2nd and 25th Divisions in the southwest sector drove northwest across the peninsula on three roughly parallel roads toward Kunsan; the 1st Cavalry Division and the rebuilt 24th Division in the central sector crossed the Naktong River near Waegwan and attacked northwest up the road to Taejon and beyond; and the six ROK divisions in the northeast sector pushed northward into the Taebaek Mountains and along the east coast road.

Military historian Clay Blair likens the 8th Army's breakout to a standing joke about the old cavalry tactics, in which "the soldiers went out and charged in all directions at the same time, with a pistol in each hand and a saber in the other." In proper military terminology, Blair goes on to note, the breakout would be worded "an attack to unlimited objectives."[78] In any event, the breakout bogged down for several days but began gathering momentum when news of the Inchon invasion started filtering down to the NK troops in the south.

Back at Inchon, Colonel Litzenberg's late-arriving 7th Marines came ashore and took up positions west of Seoul, while Murray's 5th Marines were securing the airfield at Kimpo on September 17. The next day, marine Corsairs began to operate out of the liberated field.

That same day, the 32nd Infantry Regiment of Major General David G. Barr's 7th Infantry Division debarked at the port city, with the rest of the division to follow. The 32nd Regiment moved inland to the right of the 1st Marines. They turned south in blocking positions to protect the rear of the marines. The rest of the 7th Division soon joined them. It would also serve as an "anvil" upon which the "hammer" of Walker's advancing 8th Army would pound the NKPA to pieces if all went according to plan.

By September 19, Chesty Puller's 1st Marines had secured Yongdung-p'o. They launched an abortive attempt to cross the Han River into Seoul. They tried again the next day and succeeded, as did Murray's 5th Marines, west of the city. On the morning of September 21, both regiments stood poised for the assault on Seoul. That same day, 10th Corps formally took over responsibility for Operation Chromite from Task Force Seven, and command passed from Admiral Struble to General Almond. The 10th Corps had by then offloaded 50,000 troops, 250,000 tons of equipment, and 6,000 vehicles.

MacArthur returned to his headquarters in Tokyo, leaving a parting word with Almond to take Seoul as soon as possible. Almond conferred at once with the marine commander, O.P. Smith. What MacArthur wanted, Almond said, was the liberation of Seoul by September 25, "exactly three months after the date that the North Koreans invaded South Korea."[79] The date would make for great public relations in the media but did not speak to the reality of the situation. Smith was a realist. He saw no good reason to endanger his troops by committing them to a schedule based on publicity considerations.

"I told [Almond] that I couldn't guarantee anything; that was up to the enemy," he said later. "We'd do the best we could and go as fast as we could."[80] But Smith's answer did not deter Almond. He continued to press Smith to speed up his operations. Almond even went around Smith to issue attack orders directly to Ray Murray and Chesty Puller, which did not endear him to Smith, who snapped, "You give your orders to me, and I'll see that they're carried out."[81] Almond apologized to Smith, but his breach of professional conduct did not bode well for their relationship in the weeks ahead.

A later comment in Smith's diary reflected his fury. If Almond felt it necessary to goad the marines into action, "he displayed a complete ignorance of the fighting qualities of marines."[82] The marines did enter Seoul on September 25, the date set by MacArthur for the city's liberation, but four days of hard fighting lay ahead of them.

The North Koreans had recovered quickly from the shock of the Inchon invasion. By chance, the new, but inexperienced, NK 18th Division of about 10,000 men had been passing through Seoul on the way to the Pusan Perimeter at the time of the landing. It remained to defend the city. The enemy also rushed up four independent regiments from the south—the 25th, 28th, 70th, and 87th— each with about 2,500 men. Additional forces of some 15,000 troops, including engineers and military police, brought the total number of defenders facing the UN forces in Seoul to about 35,000 or 40,000.

A helicopter takes off with wounded soldiers near Seoul in late September 1950. Bitter retaliation and resistance between North and South Korean troops resulted in many wounded and dead, both within the military and among the civilian population.

Beginning on September 21, the marines battled in close combat with the well-positioned NK defenders for the next four days, among the low hills and caves along the western approaches to Seoul. Litzenberg's 7th Marines joined their division mates on the left flank of the 5th Marines with a mission to drive across the northern reaches of Seoul and to block escape avenues to the north. A regiment of ROK Marines then joined the 5th and 1st Marines in a west-to-east assault on the city. The 32nd Infantry Regiment of Barr's 7th Division continued to guard the marines' right flank to the east. Blood flowed in torrents on both sides of the ridgelines, as the North Koreans held on stubbornly to their hill positions.

On September 24, First Lieutenant H.J. Smith's 206-man D Company was down to 30 riflemen and 14 men from its weapons platoon. Under the guns of the enemy on Hill 56, Smith decided that desperate times require desperate acts. He led the remnants of his company over the ridge and was killed instantly, but the rest of his marines pressed on. Twenty-six marines reached the crest. The North Koreans fought briefly then fled. In a single day, Smith's company took 178 casualties—36 killed and 142 wounded—but they had taken Hill 56. More important, they had precipitated the collapse of the enemy's ridgeline defenses. Doug Koch later said of Lieutenant Smith, "He was kind of a young, slender guy, who turned out to be a pretty good officer." [83]

On September 25, the North Koreans pulled out of their positions all along the western ridges, leaving behind 1,200 of their dead. The marines moved into Seoul from the west, and the 32nd Infantry captured Nam-san (South Mountain) in the east. The final phase of the fighting for the South Korean capital then began. That same day, General Almond, in his eagerness to meet General MacArthur's target date, prematurely announced the liberation of Seoul.

Meanwhile, Walker's 8th Army had broken out of the Pusan Perimeter and his forces were barreling northward at record speeds on all available roads. Upon finally receiving news of the UN landing at Inchon about a week after the fact, the NKPA in the south virtually fell apart. Except for a negligible scattering of guerrillas left behind, most of the NKPA either fled back across the 38th parallel or surrendered. One NK commander who chose to surrender was Lee Hak Ku.

Senior Colonel Lee Hak Ku, the former operations officer of 2nd Corps, had come south to serve as the NK

13th Division's chief of staff. Lee, after a fierce disagreement with his commanding officer over the futility of sacrificing any more of their men to a losing cause, Lee walked into a U.S. 8th Cavalry camp near Taegu and surrendered. He then willingly provided information on the state of his

"The Bitter Small Change of War"

On August 29, 1950, the British 27th Brigade arrived in Pusan from Hong Kong. The British contingent represented the first foreign troops other than Americans to come to the defense of the Republic of Korea. They included in their ranks the famed Argyll and Sutherland Highlanders. These legendary warriors were soon to become involved in what British military historian Max Hastings called "a wretched little tragedy."[*] It occurred during the U.S. 8th Army's breakout from the Pusan Perimeter.

Just before daybreak on September 23, the Highlanders, led by Major Kenneth Muir, began an ascent of the enemy-held Hill 282, about three miles below Songju. An hour later, they surprised a North Korean force at breakfast on the summit and quickly seized control of the hill. But nearby Hill 388—also held by the enemy—posed a threat to Muir's troops. With no artillery available, Muir put out white air panels to mark his position and called in an air strike. By the time a flight of American P-51 Mustang fighter-bombers arrived overhead, the North Koreans had also put out white air panels on Hill 388 to confuse the Mustang pilots. They succeeded.

The Mustangs dumped tanks of napalm on the wrong hill, engulfing it in orange flame and forcing most of Muir's Highlanders to evacuate Hill 282 to escape the flames. When the flames subsided, Muir led his survivors back up the hill, vowing that the enemy "will never drive the Argylls off this ridge." [**] A burst of fire killed him as he mounted the crest of the hill. Muir received the Victoria Cross posthumously, Great Britain's highest award for gallantry in action. The Highlanders lost 17 killed and 76 wounded, in a happenstance that Max Hastings described as "the bitter small change of war."[***]

[*] Max Hastings, *The Korean War*. New York: Simon & Schuster, 1987, p. 111.

[**] Ibid., pp. 111–112.

[***] Ibid., p. 112.

division, which had dwindled to 500 men and was no longer combat effective. Walker had suspected the sorry state of the enemy. Now, with proof, he attacked with vigor on all fronts.

On the morning of September 26, lead elements of the 7th Cavalry Regiment of the U.S. 1st Cavalry Division established contact with the 31st Infantry Regiment of Barr's 7th Division, near Osan, the site of Task Force Smith's earlier holding action. The 10th Corps–8th Army linkup was complete, and the fall of Seoul was imminent.

That afternoon, General MacArthur issued a UN communiqué announcing, also prematurely, the liberation of Seoul. It stated, in part:

> The liberation of Seoul was accomplished by a coordinated attack of X Corps troops. The attack started at 0630 hours [6:30 A.M.] with an amphibious crossing of the Han River south of Seoul by elements of the U.S. 7th Infantry Division coordinated with an attack by the 1st Marine Division to the west and north from positions along the outskirts of the city north of the Han River. . . .
>
> The coordination of air, tank, artillery and infantry fire power made possible the seizure of the enemy's defenses in Seoul with minimum casualties.[84]

The marines did most of the fighting inside the city, while Colonel Charles E. Beauchamp's 32nd Infantry Regiment and its attached ROK 17th Regiment seized Nam-san in the east end of Seoul and a pair of hills to the east of the city, respectively. Along the way, they cut off two main roads to the east and southeast. And they drew NK troops away from the hard-pressed marines, who were torturously engaged in rooting out the NK defenders, house by house, block by block, and street by street.

"Most of this grim, dirty, and dangerous work was carried out by the 1st, 5th, and 7th Marines over a three-day period following the release of the communiqués, September 26 to September 28," wrote Clay Blair. "The marine infantry was mightily supported by the thundering artillery pieces of the 11th Marines and marine close air support."[85]

Unfortunately, the big guns, bombs, and rockets not only dislodged or buried the enemy, but they also wreaked havoc upon the civilians inside the city. United Press war correspondent Rutherford Poats captured a sense of the hellish chaos:

> I followed the First Marines through the smoldering rubble of central Seoul the day after its premature "liberation." The last desperate Communist counter-attack had been hurled back during an eerie 2 A.M. battle of tanks firing at point blank range, American artillery crashing less than a city block ahead of marine lines, the echoed and re-echoed rattle of machine guns—all against the background of flaming buildings and darting shadows. . . .
>
> A tiny figure wrapped in a Marine's wool shirt stumbled down the street. Her face, arms, and legs were burned and almost eaten away by the fragments of an American white phosphorous artillery shell. She was blind, but somehow alive. She was about the size of my little girl. Three other Korean children, luckier than she, watched as the child reached the curbing, stumbled, and twice failed to climb up on the sidewalk. The kids laughed.[86]

While the fighting still raged at a high pitch, MacArthur reported that the North Koreans were fleeing the city. Chesty Puller, responding to a correspondent's question

Landing craft were used as staging areas for soldiers being transported by helicopter to and from the battlefront.

about their flight, answered, "All I know about a fleeing enemy is that there's two or three hundred out there that won't be fleeing anymore. They're dead."[87] Puller had greatly underestimated the body count. So it went until September 28, when the last pockets of enemy resistance collapsed to end the fighting.

MacArthur made a triumphant return to Seoul the next day to formally restore the city to South Korean President Syngman Rhee. Amid the sporadic crackling of distant gunfire from marine mopping-up operations against a few diehard NK defenders in parts of the city, MacArthur delivered a typically flowery speech to a throng of officials and citizens gathered at the steps of the scarred and shell-blackened National Capitol:

> By the grace of merciful Providence, our forces fighting under the standard of that greatest hope and inspiration of mankind, the United Nations, have liberated this ancient capital of Korea. It has been freed from the despotism of Communist rule and its citizens once more have the opportunity for that immutable concept of life which holds invincibly to the primacy of individual liberty and personal dignity.[88]

MacArthur waxed eloquently for several hundred more words. When finished, he turned to Rhee and said, "Mr. President, my officers and I will now resume our military duties and leave you and your government to the discharge of the civil responsibility."[89]

A moist-eyed Rhee grasped the general's hand and said, "We admire you. We love you as the savior of our race."[90] MacArthur returned to Tokyo within the hour.

Elements of the 1st Marine Division continued to drive northward toward Munsan and Uijongbu until the U.S. 1st Cavalry Division relieved them on October 7 and effectively ended Operation Chromite.

Over the course of the four-week operation, the 1st Marine Division suffered 2,450 casualties—366 killed in action, 49 deaths from wounds, 2,029 wounded in action, and six missing. The 7th Infantry Division incurred 572 battle casualties (including 166 South Koreans)—106 killed, 409 wounded, and 57 missing. NKPA forces sustained losses of 14,000 killed in action and another 7,000 captured.

In October 1950, after barely more than three months of war, MacArthur's forces had succeeded in decimating the North Korean People's Army and in ousting the invaders from South Korea. MacArthur's success at Inchon had exceeded all expectations. At the same time, that very success opened the door to a change in political objectives in Tokyo, in Washington, D.C., and at the United Nations in New York, from a return to the prewar situation to the liberation of the entire Korean Peninsula from Communist rule.

MacArthur now proposed a plan to transport the marines to the North Korean east-coast port of Wonsan for another amphibious operation aimed at the total destruction of the NKPA and the reunification of Korea under democratic rule. Both naval- and land-force commanders opposed the idea, but few raised their voices against the views of a general who had just pulled off a military miracle. As General Matthew B. Ridgway, then one of the Joint Chiefs, put it: "Had he [MacArthur] suggested that one battalion walk on water to reach the port, there might have been somebody ready to give it a try."[91] Thus one war ended and a new war began.

An attack by Chinese Communist forces on October 25, 1950, represented that country's entry into the Korean War. Chinese Premier Mao Zedong (seen here) vowed to "support the Korean people's war of liberation."

Chosin

We're not retreating. We're simply attacking in another direction.

—Major General Oliver P. Smith, commander
of the 1st Marine Division, in an interview with
reporters in Hagaru-ri, North Korea, December 1950
(quoted in Joseph H. Alexander, *A Fellowship of Valor*)

The brilliant planning and matchless execution of the Inchon landing won the first war in Korea in 1950. Unfortunately, it can be strongly argued that the ease and speed with which the operation was accomplished so surprised the Washington officials who headed the UN coalition—from the president on down—that few had given much thought as to what to do after the restoration of South Korea's sovereignty. "A worldwide public debate erupted whether or not United Nations troops should cross the 38th parallel to mop up the scattered remnants of the armed forces of North Korea,"[92] General MacArthur wrote later. Much of the world debate centered on Western concerns that UN aggressive action north of the 38th parallel might precipitate Soviet or Chinese intervention in the war.

In late September, the Joint Chiefs of Staff settled the issue. They sent MacArthur what they called "amplifying instructions as to further military action to be taken by you in Korea."[93] Their instructions stated, in part, and in no uncertain terms: "Your military objective is the destruction of the North Korean armed forces. In attaining this objective, you are authorized to conduct military operations north of the 38th parallel in Korea."[94]

MacArthur responded to the JCS's "amplifying instructions" with a plan to implement them. The bare bones of his plan called for Walker's 8th Army to drive across the 38th parallel and seize the North Korean capital of Pyongyang, while 10th Corps executed an amphibious landing at Wonsan, "making juncture with the Eighth Army."[95] The JCS approved MacArthur's plan on September 30.

Also on the last day of September 1950, Chinese Foreign Minister Chou En-lai announced: "The Chinese people will absolutely not tolerate foreign aggression, nor will they supinely tolerate seeing their neighbors savagely invaded by the imperialists."[96]

Just as the North Koreans had not believed that the free world would fight to preserve the tiny democracy of South Korea, the free world now refused to believe that the People's Republic of China (Red, or Communist, China) would fight to maintain the Communist regime of its tiny North Korean neighbor. But Red China was already preparing to halt UN "aggressions." And a whole new war was set to begin.

In yet another significant development on September 30, South Korean President Syngman Rhee immediately seized upon the opportunity to reunite the two Koreas under a single democratic rule—his own. He sent elements of the ROK 3rd Division crashing across the frontier in the Kangnung area in pursuit of the fleeing remnants of the NKPA: "Where is the 38th parallel? . . . It is nonexistent," he said. "I am going all the way to the Yalu [the river separating northeast China and North Korea], and the United Nations can't stop me."[97] Other ROK divisions followed a few days later. The ROK 1st Corps (3rd and Capital Divisions) soon began to average about 15 miles (24 kilometers) a day in their advance toward Wonsan, and captured the port city on September 10. Elsewhere, events moved rapidly.

On October 4, in Beijing, Chinese Premier Mao Zedong decided to intervene in the war in behalf of Kim Il Sung's North Korean regime. Four days later, Mao issued the official order to enter the war. It began:

> In order to support the Korean people's war of liberation and to resist the attacks of U.S. imperialism and its running dogs, thereby safeguarding the interests of the people of Korea, China, and all the other countries in the East, I herewith order the name of the Northeast Frontier Force changed to the Chinese People's Volunteers [hereafter called Chinese Communist Forces, or CCF] . . . to march speedily to Korea and join the Korean comrades in fighting the aggressors and winning a glorious victory.[98]

Six days later, unknown to the United Nations Command, the CCF began infiltrating large units into North Korea.

On October 7, in New York, the UN General Assembly passed a resolution authorizing the use of UN forces anywhere north of the 38th parallel for the purpose of establishing a unified and democratic Korea.

On October 9, in South Korea, the U.S. 8th Army's recently activated 1st Corps, spearheaded by the 1st Cavalry Division, crossed the 38th parallel north of Kaesong and attacked northward toward Pyongyang, with orders to press on toward the Yalu River. That same day, the 1st Marine Division began embarking at Inchon for a sea movement to Wonsan, while the 7th Infantry Division motored 350 miles (563 kilometers) to Pusan to board ship for Iwon, 100 miles (161 kilometers) farther north.

Then, on October 15, President Truman summoned General MacArthur to Wake Island, in the mid-Pacific, for a conference to discuss the military situation in Korea and an approach to the postwar rehabilitation of the small nation. MacArthur, brimming with optimism about the war's progress, told Truman, "It will be over by Thanksgiving. I hope we will be able to withdraw the Eighth Army almost immediately into Japan, probably by Christmas."[99] When Truman asked about the chances of China's intervening, MacArthur replied, "Very little."[100] Even as he spoke, however, Chinese infiltration had begun.

By October 20, CCF commander General Peng Dehuai and four 30,000-man field armies had crossed the Yalu into North Korea. Peng positioned three in western Korea, soon to oppose U.S. 8th Army and ROK forces; he placed the 4th Division in eastern Korea in what was soon to become the U.S. 10th Corps sector. Two more divisions would join Peng's forces before the end of the month.

In the meantime, the ROK Capital Division in the east had pressed northward and captured Hamhung and its port city of Hungnam, 50 air miles (81 kilometers) north of Wonsan, on October 17, and continued its drive

President Truman and General MacArthur met at Wake Island in October 1950 to discuss Korea's postwar rehabilitation.

toward the Yalu to capture Iwon, 100 miles farther up the east coast. Two days later in the west, the North Korean capital of Pyongyang fell to the U.S. 1st Cavalry and ROK 1st Divisions. That same day, October 19, General MacArthur ordered 10th Corps to move north along the east coast toward the Yalu.

On October 25, elements of the Chinese 50th Field Army launched its first offensive against the ROK 6th Division north of Unsan in west-central North Korea, about 50 air miles south of the Yalu. This attack offered the first sign of China's entry into the war. The next day, the 1st Marine Division started debarking at Wonsan. Three days later, the U.S. 7th Infantry Division began landing at Iwon.

The first significant encounter between U.S. and

Chinese troops erupted around dusk near the village of Unsan on November 1. The Chinese 39th Army's 116th Division surprised the 8th Cavalry Regiment of the U.S. 1st Cavalry Division and the 15th Regiment of the ROK 1st Division. In the battle that marked the first official recognition of Chinese intervention, Chinese forces inflicted serious losses on U.S. and ROK troops and forced their hasty withdrawal. The Chinese then disappeared into the mountains. Despite the humbling defeat, UN intelligence sources dismissed the encounter as the work of volunteers and as such lacking in military significance.

Also on November 1—while Chesty Puller's 1st Marines engaged NKPA forces in fierce fighting for Kojo, just south of Wonsan, and for the vital crossroads town of Majon-ni, 28 miles (45 kilometers) west of Wonsan—General O.P. Smith sent the main body of the 1st Marine Division northward to relieve the ROK 1st Corps at the Chosin Reservoir.

"Chosin" is the Japanese name for the reservoir called "Changjin" by the Koreans; but since "Chosin" rhymes with "frozen," the marines, for reasons that will soon become clear, preferred to use the Japanese name, as they still do more than half a century later. By either name, the reservoir, whose western shoreline lies 78 miles (126 kilometers) northwest of the port of Hungnam, is the site of a vital hydroelectric facility. A one-lane, twisting gravel road that winds through the towering Taebaek Mountains provided the only land access to the reservoir. Its serpentine path passes through the villages of Sudong-ni and Chinhung-ni, then narrows on its winding way through the treacherous Funchilin Pass to Koto-ri and on to Hagaru-ri, on the southern shore of the reservoir. Although marine infantrymen could make their way through the craggy Taebaeks on foot,

their tanks, trucks, jeeps, and artillery would be road-
blocked all the way to the Yalu and thus constantly open
to enemy attack from the mountains that lined either
side of the road. Added to terrain difficulties, the
marines were entering into one of the coldest winters
ever recorded in Korea.

Colonel Homer L. Litzenberg's 7th Marines, the fresh-
est of the three marine regiments, led the way north
and immediately ran afoul of the veteran Chinese 124th
Division on November 2 at Sudong-ni. The encounter
resulted in a fierce, five-day battle in which the
Corsairs of Marine Air Group 12 (MAG-12) out of Wonsan
proved their worth time and again, plummeting out of
the clouds and lacing the Chinese with rockets,
machine guns, and napalm. The horrific destructive
power of napalm—jellied gasoline—sent scores of Chinese screaming to their deaths. Second Lieutenant
Joseph R. Owen of B Company described one daylight
napalm attack as

> a spectacle of awesome and terrible beauty. The
> [napalm] pods slid from the planes, tumbled across the
> ground, then exploded. Black smoke billowed and red
> flame leapt against the white snow. . . . Chinese soldiers
> were aflame, running about in frenzied circles. They
> threw themselves, flailing, into the snow.[101]

On November 7, the Chinese broke off the fighting
and simply vanished into the harsh mountainous terrain,
and the marines resumed their march. To their right, the
17th Infantry Regiment, 7th Division, paralleled their
movement. To the south, the U.S. 3rd Infantry Division had
arrived from Japan and was landing at Iwon. The 17th
Infantry reached the Yalu near its source at Hyesanjin on
November 21.

On November 24, the 7th Marines crossed 4,000-foot (1,219-meter) Toktong Pass, south of the Chosin Reservoir and west of Hagaru-ri, and descended into Yudam-ni, due west of the reservoir. Litzenberg left Fox Company behind to defend the pass.

In the west, Walker's 8th Army launched a major offensive on November 24. The Chinese 13th Army Group countered immediately the next day, launching a second-phase offensive on the 8th Army front, in which they overran Walker's forces at Chongchon and set in motion the longest retreat in American military history. To relieve the pressure on Walker's command, General Almond ordered 10th Corps to the offensive on November 27. As the war heated up, the winds howled and the temperatures plunged.

Private First Class Win Scott, a 19-year-old machine gunner with C Company, later recalled the difficulties of cold-weather fighting:

> Everything froze. Our carbines wouldn't work. Artillery rounds fell short, sometimes into our own positions. Morphine froze hard as stone—the corpsmen [navy medics] carried the syrettes [tubes that carry hypodermic needles] in their mouths to keep them thawed enough to help numb the wounded.[102]

General Sung Shih-lun, commander of the 120,000-man Chinese 9th Army Group, was ready for the marines and intended to annihilate his opponents. His held his forces in check until the night of November 27—a night of blinding snows and -20°F (-29°C) temperatures—then struck the marines with sudden fury at Yudam-ni and all along the mountain road in a dozen places as far back as Hagaru-ri. Horns blared, pyrotechnics glared, and the staccato *brr-r-r-p! brr-r-r-p!* of Communist burp guns—small submachine guns—rent the air. Tens of thousands of quilt-clad soldiers swarmed to attack out of the storm and darkness, and the Battle of the Chosin Reservoir began.

At the battle's outset, the 1st Marine Division held a series of strongpoints along the so-called Main Supply Route (a charitable name for the single-lane cow path between the reservoir and Hungnam). The 5th and 7th Marines were positioned in scattered outposts on the high ground above Yudam-ni; Fox Company, 2nd Battalion, 7th Marines held the Toktong Pass; General Smith's divisional command post (CP) occupied Hagaru-ri, at the foot of the reservoir; and the 1st Marines held the division's support base at Koto-ri. The marines temporarily conceded unmanned sectors of the Main Supply Route to the enemy.

Wave upon wave of wildly screaming Chinese engulfed and overran the marine outposts overlooking Yudam-ni, but the marines fought back and held their positions. On Hill 1282, during a brief lull in the action, machine gunner Private James Gallagher of Easy Company called to his platoon leader, First Lieutenant John Yancey: "Something you gotta see, Lieutenant."[103] The sight surprised Yancey, who was a veteran of Carlson's Raiders in World War II. He described it later:

> You get to see some strange sights in war. Here's Gallagher with this grin on his face, and what he's grinning about is this string of bodies stretching right up to the gun, with the elbow of the last one actually touching the forward leg of the tripod. "Pretty good, huh, Lieutenant?" I told him to drag in two or three of the bodies and use them like sandbags in front of his position. He thought that was a great idea.[104]

Strange sights were commonplace at Chosin. Hundreds

A surprise attack during the Battle of the Chosin Reservoir in North Korea stranded U.S. soldiers and marines in the mountains for over a week. They eventually evacuated to the coast and embarked on ships to escape.

more Chinese dead piled up in front of marine guns from Yudam-ni to Hagaru-ri, as three Chinese divisions struck the two marine regiments with overwhelming force. Despite the fierce attack, the marines held fast.

At the same time, on the eastern shore of the reservoir, a fourth Chinese division struck a regimental-size army task force trying to fight its way to Hagaru-ri and link up with the marines. The Chinese division virtually destroyed the army task force, one unit at a time. Although the soldiers fought valiantly, only 385 of the task force's 3,200-man total survived the encounter with what General Almond had earlier described as "nothing more than some remnants of Chinese divisions fleeing north."[105]

In the west, Walker's 8th Army was faring no better. Under heavy attack by the Chinese 13th Army Group, Walker ordered a general withdrawal of the 8th Army from the Chongchon River line to a new defensive line at Pyongyang on November 29. Walker ordered his 2nd Infantry Division to act as a rearguard. In the ensuing Battle of Kunu-ri (November 29–December 1), the Chinese effectively destroyed the 2nd Division. The division's history recorded the action as "a magnificent stand. . . . Even in defeat, the "Indianhead" [2nd] Division proved to be a rock which held fast, giving other units an opportunity for survival."[106] It would take months for the 2nd Division to regain combat effectiveness.

Back in the east, General Almond ordered the withdrawal of 10th Corps from the Chosin Reservoir on November 30. (10th Corps now consisted of the 1st Marine Division, the U.S. 3rd and 7th Infantry Divisions, and the ROK 1st Corps.) He told General O.P. Smith to escape to the sea as fast as possible, leaving behind his heavy weapons and equipment. "No, sir," Smith replied in his quiet way. "We'll fight our way out as Marines, bringing all our weapons and gear with us."[107] When an air force general offered to evacuate the marines by air, without their heavy equipment and weapons, Smith politely turned him down.

With the Main Supply Route cut in a dozen places and the Chinese threatening to roll back the 5th and 7th Marines at Yudam-ni and overrun Smith's CP at Hagaru-ri, the marines would have to fight their way to the sea, or, as Smith himself put it, attack "in another direction." While Captain William E. Barber's encircled Fox Company held the Toktong Pass for five days, the 5th and 7th Marines stayed off the Main Supply Route and fought through the mountains to reach the pass. They found hundreds of dead Chinese in dangerously close proximity to Fox Company's lines. Barber had lost more than half of his company defending the pass, but Fox had held. Sergeant Pat Scully put it simply: "They told us to keep the pass open, and we kept it open." [108] The Yudam-ni and Toktong marines completed the 14-mile (23-kilometer) trek to Hagaru-ri on December 4.

In the meantime, Chesty Puller, commander of the 1st Marines, had sent a 900-man relief force northward from Koto-ri, headed by British marine commander Lieutenant Colonel Donald S. Drysdale. The Chinese contested "Task Force Drysdale" at every pass and gorge, captured 300 UN troops, and wounded many others. Only 300 troops made it through to Hagaru-ri. A few survivors returned to Koto-ri.

At Hagaru-ri, the marines flew out 4,316 casualties and flew in 537 replacements from a tiny airstrip that engineers had constructed in 12 days. The marine breakout from Hagaru-ri got under way on December 6, 1950. Over the next 38 hours, with marine infantrymen clearing the mountains on either side of the Main Supply Route, roughly 10,000 troops and 1,000 vehicles trudged and motored the 11 miles (18 kilometers) to Koto-ri. Staff Sergeant Lee Bergee of Easy Company recalled their arrival:

Marines of the 1st Marine Division are seen here at the airstrip near Chosin Reservoir with parachute packs to drop supplies to marines fighting nearby.

When the 5th and 7th Marines finally fought their way through to Koto-ri, planes used this runway [which engineers had also constructed earlier] to take out the casualties by the hundreds. Many of these casualties were, of course, wounded, but many others suffered from frostbite and intestinal disorders caused from eating frozen C rations and snow. Many of the latter suffered from diarrhea. Some men evacuated had pneumonia.[109]

While the evacuations took place under constant enemy fire, General Smith made plans to circumvent two major obstacles about 10 miles (16 kilometers) south of Koto-ri: a blown bridge at Funchilin Pass and an enemy strongpoint on the heights above the pass known simply as the Big Hill.

An airdrop of eight 2,500-pound (1,134-kilogram) sections of a large treadway bridge took care of the first problem. The 1st Battalion, 7th Marines, attacked southward to seize the approaches to the pass, while the 1st Battalion, 1st Marines, at Chinhung-ni attacked northward. Their combined effort eliminated the second problem, and the march to the sea continued on December 9.

"As we progressed through the pass, the high bank on our right gradually leveled off even with the road, revealing a sheer drop of 2,000 to 3,000 feet," war correspondent N. Harry Smith wrote later. "The road bank to our left rose in straight perpendicular line for hundreds of feet, against which both men and vehicles clung in shrinking terror."[110] At 1:00 P.M., on December 11, 1950, the last battered elements of General Oliver P. Smith's 1st Marine Division passed through the lines of the perimeter held by the U.S. 3rd Infantry Division around Hungnam—and the Battle of the Chosin Reservoir ended.

Marine corps losses during the entire operation consisted of 604 killed in action, another 114 who died of wounds, 192 missing in action, 3,508 wounded, and 7,313 nonbattle casualties, mostly frostbite victims. Estimated enemy losses numbered 1,500 killed and 7,500 wounded by marine ground forces, plus 10,000 killed and 5,000 wounded by marine air support. Military analysts credit the 1st Marine Division with decimating the 120,000-man Chinese 9th Army Group so as to render it incapable of interfering with the subsequent evacuation of the 10th Corps at Hungnam, or of taking part in the Chinese initial offensive into South Korea that commenced at year's end.

In contrast to the 8th Army's forced retirement in the west, most military observers characterize the Marine Corps' fighting withdrawal from the "Frozen Chosin" as a major victory over a vastly numerically superior enemy force.

Brigadier General S.L.A. Marshall, an acclaimed army historian, summed up the marines' march to the sea: "No other operation in the American book of war quite compares with this show by the 1st Marine Division in the perfection of tactical concepts precisely executed, in accuracy of estimation of the situation, in leadership at all levels, and in promptness of utilization of all supporting forces."[111]

On December 15, the marines completed embarkation at Hamhung and sailed for Pusan, not to return home for Christmas, but rather to rejoin the U.S. 8th Army and resume fighting. General of the Army Douglas MacArthur, supreme commander of UN forces, later wrote in his memoirs: "This was a new war against the vast military potential of Red China."[112] The "new war" would last for two and a half more years.

Remembering the "Forgotten War"

The last steps of the Korean War played out on July 27, 1953, in a wood-and-thatch building where representatives of the UN, North Korea, and China signed cease-fire agreements. To this day, however, no official treaty has called a formal end to the war.

[R]egardless of our having missed "total victory" in Korea (if any such consummation could ever have been found there), we did deliver to international Communism its first resounding defeat.

—General Matthew B. Ridgway, supreme commander of
UN forces in Korea, 1951–1952 (in *The Korean War*)

O n July 27, 1953, the faint rumble of heavy artillery and the spasmodic chattering of small-arms fire could be heard up and down the front lines until sundown, when the weapons of war fell silent. Only then did the frontline troops fully accept the notion that the long-promised end of the war was truly only hours away. At 10:12 A.M., after more than two years of negotiations, representatives of both sides had finally agreed upon a truce. The armistice was set to begin at 10:00 P.M., less than 12 hours later.

Shortly after 9:00 P.M., U.S. marines occupying positions along the main line of resistance near Panmunjom sighted a group of Chinese digging trenches no more than 100 yards (91 meters) in front of them. Their battalion commander, Lieutenant Colonel Joseph Hill, issued orders not to shoot. "Don't start anything you can't stop,"[113] he cautioned. Exercising their traditionally strict discipline, the marines held their fire. They instead settled for throwing rocks at the enemy for the final 40 minutes of the war.

The armistice commenced at the top of the hour sharp. The war that had begun 37 months before as a "police action," but had subsequently escalated into one of the bloodiest wars in America's history, had ended at last. Ironically, it ended just about where it had begun along the 38th parallel. The status quo had been restored, however, and peace prevailed once again in the Land of the Morning Calm. Because of the courage and sacrifices of the armed forces of 16 nations fighting under the blue and white banner of the United Nations, the Republic of (South) Korea and its people remained free.

In defense of a nearly defenseless friend, the UN forces had borne a huge burden and overcome countless hardships to assure the liberty of a tiny nation. But the price of freedom was high. The United States suffered losses of 54,246 dead (33,629 killed in action; 20,617 military dead from accidents and other causes) and 103,284 wounded. Pentagon records list the total UN casualties—dead, wounded, and missing—as 996,937, of whom 850,000 were ROKs, and 17,000 were from nations other than the United States. Communist forces killed, wounded, or missing totaled 1.42 million, including 520,000 NKPA. Added to these figures were an estimated 2 million North and South

The human aftermath of war can be seen in this image of a widowed father of four who labors to build a shelter for his family on the ruins of his former home.

Korean civilian casualties, bringing the overall count of devastated human lives to an appalling 4.4 million. Now, more than half a century later, they—and the war that claimed them—are all but forgotten.

Of all the major wars fought by the United States throughout its history, the Korean War, for whatever reason, is the least remembered. Although it ranks near the top in terms of world impact and importance—and certainly in casualties—it dwells only marginally in the American (and global) consciousness.

Sandwiched between World War II and the Vietnam War—America's largest and fiercest war, and its most unpopular and protested war, respectively—the Korean

The Yin and Yang of the Korean War

The Korean War of 1950–1953 has frequently been called the "forgotten war" and not without good reason. In the more than five decades since the start of the conflict, two generations of otherwise preoccupied Americans have all but forgotten why President Truman sent U.S. forces there in the first place, or what they accomplished while they were there. Had it not been for the popular television series *M.A.S.H.*, many Americans would know little or nothing about the Korean War. (Ironically, *M.A.S.H.* represented more of an antiwar "statement" against the Vietnam War than a faithful portrayal of the Korean War.)

Yet, despite being quickly relegated to its "forgotten" status, the Korean War had a colossal impact on the lives of millions of people across the globe. As stated in a historical document by the U.S. secretary of defense, the Korean War "had as much to do with shaping the world of the second half of the twentieth century as did World War II."*

Perhaps the war's greatest impact was felt—and is still being felt—among the people of the Republic of (South) Korea. To them, the "forgotten war" is likely to be remembered as long as the forces of yin and yang control the universe. In Far Eastern philosophy, *yin* (feminine force) and *yang* (masculine force) together represent the principles of the universe. Their complementary symbols form a part of the flag that yet waves proudly over the *free* Republic of Korea.

* Quoted in Stanley Sandler, *The Korean War: No Victors, No Vanquished*. Lexington, KY: University Press of Kentucky, 1999, p. ix.

War seems somehow to have been lost in the transition from a war fought clearly for all the right reasons, and one fought—equally clearly, now—for all the wrong reasons. In the early 1950s, the American public saw the Korean War and the reason it was fought as neither white nor black, but as the drab, neutral color of gray, which made it much more forgettable.

Nonetheless, the Korean War set a precedent, a standard, for the despots of the world to remember. Today, in an increasingly dangerous world, any would-be aggressor who might choose to threaten the sovereignty of the Republic of Korea would do well to contemplate the words of American General Matthew B. Ridgway: "The conclusion of the armistice found the sixteen allies with combat forces in Korea solemnly reaffirming their resolve to respond promptly if the aggression should be renewed and, in that event, not necessarily limit themselves to operations on the Korean Peninsula." [114]

1950

June 25	North Korean People's army (NKPA) crosses over 38th parallel and invades Republic of (South) Korea (ROK). United Nations (UN) Security Council calls for North Korea to end aggression and recall the NKPA.
June 27	President Harry Truman authorizes U.S. air and naval operations south of 38th parallel to support ROK forces. UN Security Council adopts U.S. resolution proclaiming NKPA attack a breach of world peace.
June 28	Seoul falls to NKPA.
June 29	President Truman authorizes sea blockade of the Korean coast and bombing of North Korea.
June 30	President Truman authorizes commitment of U.S. ground forces to combat in Korea.
July 5	Task Force Smith of the 24th Infantry Division engages and delays NKPA forces at Osan in first U.S. ground action of the war.
July 7	UN Security Council asks the United States to act as its executive agent and to organize a United Nations Command (UNC) to prosecute the war.
July 8	President Truman names General of the Army Douglas MacArthur to head UNC.
July 13	Lieutenant General Walton H. Walker arrives at Taegu from Japan and establishes forward headquarters of U.S. 8th Army.
July 29	General Walker issues "stand or die" order to U.S. 8th Army.
August 4	Pusan (Naktong) Perimeter established.
August 7	1st Provisional Marine Brigade committed to combat at Chinju.
August 8–18	First Battle of the Naktong Bulge.
August 15–20	Battle of the Bowling Alley.
August 16	10th Corps activated under Major General Edward M. "Ned" Almond to control Inchon invasion force.
August 31– September 19	Second Battle of the Naktong Bulge.
September 15	D day for Inchon invasion by Joint Task Force Seven.
September 27	Seoul liberated by 1st Marine Division and U.S. 7th Infantry Division and attached forces.

September 30	ROK 3rd Division crosses 38th parallel in pursuit of fleeing NKPA.
October 7	UN General Assembly passes resolution authorizing use of UN troops anywhere north of 38th parallel to establish unified and democratic Korea.
October 9	Elements of U.S. 8th Army cross 38th parallel and attack northward toward North Korean capital of Pyongyang.
October 14–20	Chinese Communist Forces (CCF) commence secret infiltration into North Korea.
October 26–28	1st Marine Division lands at Wonsan on east coast of Korea.
October 2– November 9	U.S. 7th Infantry Division lands at Iwon, 150 miles north of Wonsan.
November 2–7	7th Marine Regiment engages CCF 124th Division at Sudong.
November 5–17	U.S. 3rd Infantry Division lands at Wonsan.
November 21	17th Infantry Regiment, 7th Division, reaches Yalu River near its source near Hyesanjin in eastern Korea.
November 24	U.S. 8th Army launches major offensive in western Korea.
November 25	Chinese 13th Army Group counterattacks with second phase offensive on 8th Army front.
November 27	10th Corps attacks in the east to relieve pressure on 8th Army in the west.
November 27– December 11	Battle of the Chosin Reservoir.
November 29	General Walker orders general withdrawal of 8th Army in western Korea.
November 29– December 1	Battle of Kunu-ri.
November 30	General Almond orders withdrawal of 10th Corps to Hungnam.
December 9	General MacArthur orders evacuation of 10th Corps from Hungnam.
December 24	Evacuation of 10th Corps completed at Hungnam.
December 31, 1950– January 5, 1951	Chinese Communist Forces launch third-phase offensive.
1953	
July 27	Armistice in Korean War commences.

CHAPTER 1: THE SOUND OF THUNDER

1. Quoted in Clay Blair, *The Forgotten War: America in Korea 1950–1953*. New York: Times Books, 1987, p. 56.
2. Quoted in T.R. Fehrenbach, *This Kind of War: The Classic Korean War History*. Washington, D.C.: Brassey's, 1994, p. 8.
3. Quoted in Blair, p. 56.
4. Quoted in Fehrenbach, p. 11.

CHAPTER 2: THE ORIGINS OF THE KOREAN WAR

5. Quoted in Sergei N. Goncharov, John W. Lewis, and Xue Litai, *Uncertain Partners: Stalin, Mao, and the Korean War*. Stanford, CA: Stanford University Press, 1993, p. 2.
6. Quoted in Robert Leckie, *Conflict: The History of the Korean War, 1950–53*. New York: Da Capo Press, 1996, p. 31.
7. Ibid.
8. Goncharov, Lewis, and Litai, p. 2.
9. Quoted in Norman Polmar and Thomas B. Allen, *World War II: The Encyclopedia of the War Years 1941–1945*. New York: Random House, 1996, p. 654.
10. Ronald Grigor Suny, *The Soviet Experiment: Russia, the USSR, and the Successor States*. New York: Oxford University Press, 1998, p. 345.
11. Quoted in Joseph C. Goulden, *Korea: The Untold Story of the War*. New York: Times Books, 1982, p. 19.
12. Ibid.
13. Ibid.
14. John Toland, *In Mortal Combat: Korea, 1950–1953*. New York: William Morrow, 1991, p. 16.
15. Ibid.

CHAPTER 3: THE FIRST SIX WEEKS

16. Quoted in Max Hastings, *The Korean War*. New York: Simon & Schuster, 1987, p. 53.
17. Quoted in Robert Leckie, *The Wars of America*, vol. 2. New York: HarperCollins, 1993, p. 851.
18. Quoted in Robert J. Dvorchak, and the writers and photographers of the Associated Press, *Battle for Korea: The Associated Press History of the Korean Conflict*. Conshohocken, PA: Combined Books, 1993, p. 9.
19. Quoted in Stanley Weintraub, *MacArthur's War: Korea and the Undoing of an American Hero*. New York: Free Press, 2000, p. 39.
20. Quoted in Dvorchak, pp. 10–11.
21. Quoted in Leckie, p. 54.
22. Quoted in William Manchester, *American Caesar: Douglas MacArthur 1880–1964*. Boston: Little, Brown, 1978, p. 554.
23. Ibid., p. 555.
24. Quoted in Leckie, p. 56.
25. Ibid., p. 57.
26. Quoted in Bevin Alexander, *Korea: The First War We Lost*. New York: Hippocrene Books, 1986, p. 33.
27. Quoted in John Toland, *In Mortal Combat: Korea, 1950–1953*. New York: William Morrow, 1991, p. 59.
28. Quoted in Hastings, p. 73.
29. Quoted in Manchester, p. 559.
30. Quoted in Alexander, p. 55.
31. Quoted in T.R. Fehrenbach, *This Kind of War: The Classic Korean War History*. Washington, D.C.: Brassey's, 1994, p. 77.
32. Quoted in Leckie, pp. 63–64.
33. Quoted in Donald Knox, *The Korean War: Pusan to Chosin*. Orlando, FL: Harcourt Brace, 1985, p. 20.
34. Ibid., pp. 24–25.
35. Quoted in Spencer Tucker, "Task Force Smith," in *The Korean War: An Encyclopedia*, ed. by Stanley Sandler. New York: Garland Publishing, 1995, p. 330.
36. Quoted in Knox, p. 40.
37. Quoted in Leckie, p. 95.

CHAPTER 4: THE PUSAN PERIMETER

38. Quoted in Joseph C. Goulden, *Korea: The Untold Story of the War*. New York: Times Books, 1982, p. 175.
39. Quoted in Robert Leckie, *Conflict: The History of the Korean War, 1950–1953*. New York: Da Capo Press, 1996, p. 101.
40. Lynn Montross and Nicholas A. Canzona, "Chapter 6, Action on Hill 342, First Platoon Fight," in *U.S. Marine Operations in Korea*, vol. 1 (hereafter USMC-1), *The Pusan Perimeter* (part of CD-ROM *The Sea Services in the Korean War 1950–1953*), p. 2.
41. Quoted in John Toland, *In Mortal Combat: Korea, 1950–1953*. New York: William Morrow, 1991, pp. 136–137.
42. Montross and Canzona, p. 3.
43. Quoted in Donald Knox, *The Korean War: Pusan to Chosin*. Orlando, FL: Harcourt Brace, 1985, pp. 119–120.
44. Quoted in J. Robert Moskin, *The Story of the United States Marine Corps*, 3rd rev. ed. Boston: Little, Brown, 1992, p. 453.
45. Ibid., p. 454.
46. Quoted in Goulden, p. 177.
47. Ibid.
48. Ibid.
49. Quoted in Joseph H. Alexander, with Don Horan and Norman C. Stahl, *A Fellowship of Valor: The Battle History of the United States Marines*. New York: HarperCollins, 1997, p. 262.

50. Ibid.
51. Quoted in Robert J. Dvorchak, and the writers and photographers of the Associated Press, *Battle for Korea: The Associated Press History of the Korean Conflict.* Conshohocken, PA: Combined Books, 1993, p. 37.
52. Ibid., p. 43.
53. Quoted in Leckie, p. 114.

CHAPTER 5: INCHON

54. Douglas MacArthur, *Reminiscences: General of the Army Douglas MacArthur.* Annapolis, MD: Naval Institute Press, 2001, pp. 332–333.
55. Ibid., p. 333.
56. Quoted in Joseph C. Goulden, *Korea: The Untold Story of the War.* New York: Times Books, 1982, p. 185.
57. Ibid., p. 186.
58. MacArthur, p. 350.
59. Ibid.
60. Ibid.
61. Ibid.
62. Ibid.
63. Ibid., p. 351.
64. Quoted in Bevin Alexander, *How Great Generals Win.* New York: W.W. Norton, 2002, p. 284.
65. Quoted in Stanley Sandler, *The Korean War: No Victors, No Vanquished.* Lexington, KY: University Press of Kentucky, 1999, p. 91.
66. Quoted in Robert Leckie, *Conflict: The History of the Korean War, 1950–1953.* New York: Da Capo Press, 1996, p. 140.
67. Quoted in Joseph H. Alexander, with Don Horan and Norman C. Stahl, *A Fellowship of Valor: The Battle History of the United States Marines.* New York: HarperCollins, 1997, p. 270.
68. Quoted in John Toland, *In Mortal Combat: Korea, 1950–1953.* New York: William Morrow, 1991, p. 195.
69. Quoted in Donald Knox, *The Korean War: Pusan to Chosin.* Orlando, FL: Harcourt Brace, 1985, p. 240.
70. Ibid.
71. Quoted in Leckie, p. 142.
72. Ibid.

CHAPTER 6: SEOUL

73. Quoted in Donald Knox, *The Korean War: Pusan to Chosin.* Orlando, FL: Harcourt Brace, 1985, p. 262.
74. Quoted in John Toland, *In Mortal Combat: Korea, 1950–1953.* New York: William Morrow, 1991, pp. 201–202.
75. Quoted in Stanley Weintraub, *MacArthur's War: Korea and the Undoing of an American Hero.* New York: Free Press, 2000, p. 138.

76. Ibid.
77. Quoted in Knox, p. 281.
78. Quoted in Clay Blair, *The Forgotten War: America in Korea 1950–1953.* New York: Times Books, 1987, p. 278.
79. Quoted in Joseph C. Goulden, *Korea: The Untold Story of the War.* New York: Times Books, 1982, p. 226.
80. Ibid.
81. Quoted in Joseph H. Alexander, with Don Horan and Norman C. Stahl, *A Fellowship of Valor: The Battle History of the United States Marines.* New York: HarperCollins, 1997, p. 278.
82. Quoted in Goulden, p. 227.
83. Quoted in Knox, p. 176.
84. Quoted in Shelby L. Stanton, *America's Tenth Legion: X Corps in Korea, 1950.* Novato, CA: Presidio Press, 1989, pp. 105–106.
85. Blair, p. 293.
86. Quoted in Robert Leckie, *Conflict: The History of the Korean War, 1950–1953.* New York: Da Capo Press, 1996, pp. 151–152.
87. Quoted in Weintraub, p. 152.
88. Quoted in Goulden, p. 230.
89. Ibid.
90. Ibid.
91. Ibid., p. 232.

CHAPTER 7: CHOSIN

92. Douglas MacArthur, *Reminiscences: General of the Army Douglas MacArthur.* Annapolis, MD: Naval Institute Press, 2001, p. 358.
93. Ibid.
94. Ibid.
95. Ibid.
96. Quoted in Robert Leckie, *Conflict: The History of the Korean War, 1950–1953.* New York: Da Capo Press, 1996, p. 153.
97. Ibid.
98. Quoted in Sergei N. Goncharov, John W. Lewis, and Xue Litai, *Uncertain Partners: Stalin, Mao, and the Korean War.* Stanford, CA: Stanford University Press, 1993, p. 184.
99. Quoted in Stanley Weintraub, *MacArthur's War: Korea and the Undoing of an American Hero.* New York: Free Press, 2000, p. 189.
100. Quoted in Harry G. Summers, Jr., *Korean War Almanac.* New York: Facts on File, 1990, p. 298.
101. Quoted in Joseph H. Alexander, with Don Horan and Norman C. Stahl, *A Fellowship of Valor: The Battle History of the United States Marines.* New York: HarperCollins, 1997, p. 286.
102. Ibid., p. 287.
103. Quoted in Martin Russ, *Breakout: The Chosin Reservoir Campaign, Korea 1950.* New York: Fromm International, 1999, p. 138.
104. Ibid.

105. Quoted in T. R. Fehrenbach, *This Kind of War: The Classic Korean War History*. Washington, D.C.: Brassey's, 1994, p. 290.

106. Quoted in Max Hastings, *The Korean War*. New York: Simon & Schuster, 1987, pp. 144–145.

107. Quoted in Alexander, *A Fellowship of Valor*, p. 294.

108. Quoted in Rudy Tomedi, *No Bugles, No Drums: An Oral History of the Korean War*. New York: John Wiley & Sons, 1993, p. 84.

109. Quoted in Donald Knox, *The Korean War: Pusan to Chosin*. Orlando, FL: Harcourt Brace, 1985, p. 583.

110. Ibid., p. 605.

111. Quoted in Alexander, *A Fellowship of Valor*, p. 301.

112. MacArthur, p. 377.

CHAPTER 8: REMEMBERING THE "FORGOTTEN WAR"

113. Quoted in Joseph C. Goulden, *Korea: The Untold Story of the War*. New York: Times Books, 1982, p. 645.

114. Matthew B. Ridgway, *The Korean War*. New York: Da Capo Press, 1967, p. 240.

BOOKS

Alexander, Bevin. *How Great Generals Win*. New York: W.W. Norton, 2002.

———. *Korea: The First War We Lost*. New York: Hippocrene Books, 1986.

Alexander, Joseph H., with Don Horan and Norman C. Stahl. *A Fellowship of Valor: The Battle History of the United States Marines*. New York: HarperCollins, 1997.

Blair, Clay. *The Forgotten War: America in Korea 1950–1953*. New York: Times Books, 1987.

———. *MacArthur*. Garden City, NY: Nelson Doubleday, 1977.

Davis, Paul K. *100 Decisive Battles: From Ancient Times to the Present*. New York: Oxford University Press, 1999.

Deane, Hugh. *The Korean War 1945–1953*. San Francisco: China Books, 1999.

Dupuy, R. Ernest, and Trevor N. Dupuy. *The Encyclopedia of Military History*. Rev. ed. New York: Harper & Row, 1977.

Dupuy, Trevor N., Curt John, and David L. Bongard. *The Harper Encyclopedia of Military Biography*. New York: HarperCollins, 1992.

Dvorchak, Robert J., and the writers and photographers of the Associated Press. *Battle for Korea: The Associated Press History of the Korean Conflict*. Conshohocken, PA: Combined Books, 1993.

Eggenberger, David. *An Encyclopedia of Battles: Accounts of over 1,560 Battles from 1479 B.C. to the Present*. New York: Dover Publications, 1985.

Ent, Uzal W. *Fighting on the Brink: Defense of the Pusan Perimeter*. Paducah, KY: Turner Publishing, 1998.

Fehrenbach, T. R. *This Kind of War: The Classic Korean War History*. Washington, DC: Brassey's, 1994.

Gailey, Harry A. *Historical Encyclopedia of the United States Marine Corps*. Lanham, MD: Scarecrow Press, 1998.

Goncharov, Sergei N., John W. Lewis, and Xue Litai. *Uncertain Partners: Stalin, Mao, and the Korean War*. Stanford, CA: Stanford University Press, 1993.

Goulden, Joseph C. *Korea: The Untold Story of the War*. New York: Times Books, 1982.

Hammel, Eric. *Chosin: Heroic Ordeal of the Korean War*. Novato, CA: Presidio Press, 1990.

Hastings, Max. *The Korean War*. New York: Simon & Schuster, 1987.

Hopkins, William B. *One Bugle, No Drums: The Marines at Chosin Reservoir*. New York: Avon Books, 1986.

Hoyt, Edwin P. *On to the Yalu*. Briarcliff Manor, NY: Stein and Day, 1984.

James, D. Clayton, with Anne Sharp Wells. *Refighting the Last War: Command and Crisis in Korea 1950–1953*. New York: Free Press, 1993.

Knox, Donald. *The Korean War: Pusan to Chosin*. Orlando, FL: Harcourt Brace, 1985.

———. with additional text by Alfred Coppel. *The Korean War: Uncertain Victory*. San Diego: Harcourt Brace Jovanovich, 1988.

Leckie, Robert. *Conflict: The History of the Korean War, 1950–53*. New York: Da Capo Press, 1996.

———. *The Wars of America*. Vol. 2. New York: HarperCollins, 1993.

MacArthur, Douglas. *Reminiscences: General of the Army Douglas MacArthur*. Annapolis, MD: Naval Institute Press, 2001.

Manchester, William. *American Caesar: Douglas MacArthur 1880–1964*. Boston: Little, Brown, 1978.

Margiotta, Franklin D., ed. *Brassey's Encyclopedia of Land Forces and Warfare*. Washington, D.C.: Brassey's, 1996.

———. *Brassey's Encyclopedia of Military History and Biography*. Washington, D.C.: Brassey's, 1994.

Matloff, Maurice, ed. *American Military History*. Vol. 2: 1902–1996. Conshohocken, PA: Combined Books, 1996.

Moskin, J. Robert. *The Story of the United States Marine Corps*. 3rd Rev. ed. Boston: Little, Brown, 1992.

Quick, John. *Dictionary of Weapons & Military Terms*. New York: McGraw-Hill, 1973.

Ridgway, Matthew B. *The Korean War*. New York: Da Capo Press, 1967.

Russ, Martin. *Breakout: The Chosin Reservoir Campaign, Korea 1950*. New York: Fromm International, 1999.

———. *The Last Parallel: A Marine's War Journal*. New York: Fromm International, 1999.

Sandler, Stanley. *The Korean War: No Victors, No Vanquished*. Lexington, KY: University Press of Kentucky, 1999.

———. *The Korean War: An Encyclopedia*. Vol. 872. New York: Garland Publishing, 1995.

Stanton, Shelby L. *America's Tenth Legion: X Corps in Korea, 1950*. Novato, CA: Presidio Press, 1989.

Stokesbury, James L. *A Short History of the Korean War*. New York: William Morrow, 1988.

Stueck, William. *The Korean War: An International History*. Princeton, NJ: Princeton University Press, 1995.

Summers, Harry G., Jr. *Korean War Almanac*. New York: Facts on File, 1990.

Suny, Ronald Grigor. *The Soviet Experiment: Russia, the USSR, and the Successor States*. New York: Oxford University Press, 1998.

Toland, John. *In Mortal Combat: Korea, 1950–1953*. New York: William Morrow, 1991.

Tomedi, Rudy. *No Bugles, No Drums: An Oral History of the Korean War*. New York: John Wiley & Sons, 1993.

Weintraub, Stanley. *MacArthur's War: Korea and the Undoing of an American Hero*. New York: Free Press, 2000.

CD-ROM

The Sea Services in the Korean War 1950–1953. Produced by the Naval Institute Press and Sonalysts, Inc., in conjunction with the historical offices of the U.S. Navy, Marine Corps, and Coast Guard. © 1957, 2000 by the U.S. Naval Institute, Annapolis, Maryland.

Boyne, Walter J. *Beyond the Wild Blue: A History of the United States Air Force 1947–1997*. New York: St. Martin's Press, 1997.

Bradley, Omar N., and Clay Blair. *A General's Life*. New York: Simon & Schuster, 1983.

Brady, James. *The Coldest War: A Memoir of Korea*. New York: Orion Books, 1990.

Bussey, Charles M. *Firefight at Yechon: Courage and Racism in the Korean War*. New York: Macmillan, 1991.

Clark, Eugene Franklin. *The Secrets of Inchon: The Untold Story of the Most Daring Covert Mission of the Korean War*. New York: G.P. Putnam's Sons, 2002.

Davis, Burke. *Marine! The Life of Chesty Puller*. Boston: Little, Brown, 1962.

Duncan, David Douglas. *This Is War! A Photo-Narrative of the Korean War*. Boston: Little, Brown, 1990.

Forty, George. *At War in Korea*. London: Arms and Armour, 1997.

Giangreco, D. M. *War in Korea 1950–1953*. Novato, CA: Presidio Press, 1990.

Hunt, George P. *The Story of the U.S. Marines*. New York: Random House, 1951.

Marshall, S.L.A. *Pork Chop Hill: The American Fighting Man in Action, Korea, Spring, 1953*. Nashville, TN: Battery Press, (Book Club Edition; no date given).

———. *The River and the Gauntlet: The Battle of the Chongchon River, Korea 1950*. Nashville: Battery Press, (Book Club Edition; no date given).

Murphy, Edward F. *Korean War Heroes*. Novato, CA: Presidio Press, 1992.

Owen, Joseph R. *Colder than Hell: A Marine Rifle Company at Chosin Reservoir*. Annapolis, MD: Naval Institute Press, 1996.

Paschall, Rod. *Witness to War: Korea*. New York: Berkley, 1995.

Remembering the Forgotten War: Korea: 1950–1953. New York: History Book Club, 2000.

Terry, Addison. *The Battle for Pusan: A Korean War Memoir*. Novato, CA: Presidio Press, 2000.

Thomas, Nigel, and Peter Abbott. *The Korean War 1950–53*. Men-at-Arms series. Edited by Martin Windrow. Oxford, UK: Osprey, 1998.

Wilson, Jim. *Retreat, Hell! We're Just Attacking in Another Direction*. New York: William Morrow, 1988.

Acheson, Dean G., 33
Alexander, Joseph H., 58
Almond, Edward M. "Ned," 71, 84-85, 87, 102, 105
Appleman, Roy F., 61
atomic bomb
    U.S. dropping on Hiroshima and Nagasaki, 23
    U.S. testing, 22
Attlee, Clement, 22

Badoeng Strait, U.S.S., 55
Barber, William E., 106
Barr, David G., 72, 84, 86, 89
Beauchamp, Charles E., 89
Bell, James, 57
Bergee, Lee, 83, 106-107
Big Hill, 107
Blair, Clay, 83-84, 90
Blue Beach, 73, 76, 77
Bonesteel, C.H. III, 24
Bowling Alley, Battle of the, 59-61
Bradley, Omar N., 73, 79
Brines, Russell, 36
Britain
    and Cairo Conference, 21, 26
    and Yalta Conference, 20-21
British 27th Brigade, 63
Buddhism, 25

Cairo Conference, 21-22, 26
Canzona, Nicholas A., 54-55
CCF 4th Division, 98

CCF 9th Army Group, 102, 108
CCF 13th Army, 105
CCF 39th Army, 100
CCF 50th Field Army, 99
CCF 116th Division, 100
CCF 124th Division, 101
Cemetery Hill, 77
Chiang Kai-shek (Jiang Jieshi), 14
    and Cairo Conference, 21, 26
    and concessions to Stalin, 20-21, 23
China
    and borders with Korea, 25
    and Cairo Conference, 21, 26
    and concessions to Stalin, 20-21, 23
    and United States, 34, 98
    See also Chinese Communist Forces (CCF)
Chinese Communist Forces (CCF)
    and casualties, 101, 103, 105, 106, 108
    and Chosin, 95-103, 105-109
    and entry into Korean War, 96-97, 98, 99-100
    and fighting for Soviet Union, 36-37
Chinese Eastern Railroads, 20
Chinhung-ni, 108
Chinju, 52, 53
Chochiwon, 44
Choe Yong Gun, 31, 35
Chonan (Ch'onan), 43

Chongchon, 102
Chongchon River, 105
Chosin, 95-103, 105-109
Chosin Reservoir, Battle of, 102-103, 105-108
Chou En-lai, 96
Chunchon (Ch'unch'on), 32
Churchill, Winston
    and Cairo Conference, 21, 26
    and Yalta Conference, 20-21
Church, John H., 40, 53, 56, 57
Clark, Eugene F., 74
Cold War, 20-22, 27
Collins, J. Lawton, 69-70, 71
Communists. *See* China; Democratic People's Republic of Korea; North Korean People's Army; Soviet Union
Congress
    and extension of the draft, 37
    and intervention in Korea, 37-38
Craig, Edward A., 53, 56, 57, 63, 65

Dairen (Dalian), 20
Day, Philip, Jr., 42
D day, and Inchon invasion, 71, 72-74
Dean, William F., 12-13, 39, 40, 43, 44, 45, 53
Doyle, James H., 72, 74
DPRK. *See* Democratic People's Republic of Korea
Drysdale, Donald S., 106

EUSA Forward Head-
    quarters, 44, 45

Far Eastern Command,
    and MacArthur, 14
fire brigade, 56, 63
Fleet Marine Force
    (FMF) Pacific, 68
Flying Fish Channel,
    73
Freeman, Paul L., Jr.,
    60
Funchilin Pass, 107-108

Gallagher, James, 103
General Headquarters
    Far East Command,
    71
Germany
    four-nation occupation
        of, 20
    and World War II, 22
Gibney, Frank, 13-14
Gibson, Tom, 77
Goncharov, Sergei N.,
    22
Great Naktong Offen-
    sive, 63
Green Beach, 72-73

Hagaru-ri, 102, 103,
    105, 106
Halsey, William F.
    "Bull," 79
Hamhung, 98, 109
Han River, 82, 84
Harvey, Robert, 55
Higgins, J.M., 73
Hill, John G., 57
Hill, Joseph, 112
Hill 56, 87
Hill 255, 54
Hill 303, 61
Hill 342, 54-55

Hill 1282, 103
Hiroshima, U.S. drop-
    ping atomic bomb on,
    23
Hungnam, 98, 108
Hwach'on, 12

Inchon, invasion of, 40,
    65, 67-79, 82, 93, 95-
    96
Itazuke air base, 39
Iwon, 98, 99, 101

Japan
    and Korea, 21, 25-26
    Soviet Union's entry
        into World War II
        against, 20-21, 22, 23
    and surrender in
        World War II, 19,
        23, 24
    and U.S. dropping
        atomic bombs on
        Hiroshima and
        Nagasaki, 23
    and U.S. testing
        atomic bomb, 22
Japan, Sea of, 16, 25, 50
Joint Chiefs of Staff
    (JCS)
    and Inchon invasion,
        69-71, 73, 79
    and military opera-
        tions north of 38th
        parallel, 96
Joint Task Force Seven,
    72

Kaesong, 98
Kean, William B., 52,
    53, 56
Kim Chaik, 63
Kim Il Sung, 28-29, 32,
    50, 97

Kimpo, 73, 82, 84
Koch, Doug, 82-83, 87
Kojo, 100
Korea
    division of, 26-28
    and establishment of
        38th parallel, 23-25,
        26
    geography of, 25
    history of as battle-
        ground, 25-26
    and independence, 21,
        26
    and Japan, 21, 25-26
    as Land of the Morn-
        ing Calm, 25, 29,
        112
    occupation of, 23-25,
        26
    people of, 25-26
    as puppet state of
        Soviet Union, 21-
        22, 28-29
Korean War
    and armistice, 112,
        115
    beginning of, 12-17
    casualties of, 17, 112-
        113
    and Chosin, 95-103,
        105-109
    end of, 111-112
    first six weeks of,
        31-47
    as forgotten war,
        114-115
    and Inchon, 40, 65,
        67-79, 82, 93, 95-
        96
    lesson of, 115
    origins of, 19-29
    and prevention of
        World War III,
        17

and Pusan (Naktong)
Perimeter, 38, 39,
40, 45, 47, 49-61,
51, 60, 63-65, 109
See also Seoul
Korea Strait, 25, 50
Koto-ri, 103, 106, 107
Kum River, 53
Kunsan, 70, 83
Kunu-ri, Battle of, 105

Land of the Morning
Calm, 25, 29, 112
Lee Hak Ku, 12, 15, 17,
87-89
Lewis, John W., 22
Litzenberg, Homer L.,
82, 84, 86, 101, 102
Lopez, Baldomero, 76-
77

MacArthur, Douglas,
50
and bravery, 82-83
and China, 109
and display of
strength, 38-39
and Far Eastern
Command, 14
as head of UN Com-
mand, 44
and Inchon invasion,
67-75, 79, 82, 93
and military opera-
tions north of 38th
parallel, 96, 98, 99
and NKPA crossing
38th parallel, 33-34
and no forced evacua-
tion from Korea,
45
and Pusan (Naktong)
Perimeter, 50, 51,
64-65

and request for full
utilization, 36, 37
and reunification of
Korea, 93
and Seoul, 84-85, 87,
89, 90, 92, 93
and troops to Korea,
44-45
and Wonson, 93
Main Supply Route, 103,
106
Majon-ni, 100
Manchuria, 20, 23
Mao Zedong, 14, 97
Marshall, George C.,
23-24, 27-28
Marshall, S.L.A., 109
Masan Front, 51, 52, 53
McCloy, John J., 24
Michaelis, John H.
"Iron Mike," 60, 61
Miryang, 56
Mongols, 25
Montross, Lynn, 54-55,
57
Mount McKinley, U.S.S.,
74
Muccio, John J., 13, 14,
33
Muchon-ni, 53
Munsan, 92
Murray, Raymond L., 58,
76, 77, 81, 82, 84, 85

Nagasaki, U.S. dropping
atomic bomb on, 23
Naktong Bulge
First Battle of the,
56-59
Second Battle of the,
63-64
Naktong Perimeter. *See*
Pusan (Naktong)
Perimeter

Naktong River, 49, 51
Nam-san (South Moun-
tain), 87, 89
napalm, and Chosin,
101
NK 1st Corps, 51
NK 1st Division, 61, 63
NK 2nd Corps, 12, 51, 87
NK 3rd Division, 59, 61,
63
NK 4th Army, 57
NK 4th Division, 41, 53,
58
NK 5th Division, 63
NK 6th Division, 52, 53,
54-55, 56
NK 9th Division, 63
NK 10th Division, 61, 63
NK 12th Division, 63
NK 13th Division, 61, 63
NK 18th Division, 85
NK 25th Division, 85
NK 28th Division, 85
NK 70th Division, 85
NK 87th Division, 85
NK 105th Armored
Brigade, 41, 42
NK 107th Tank Battal-
ion, 41
North Atlantic Treaty
Organization
(NATO), 14
North Korea. *See* Demo-
cratic People's Repub-
lic of Korea; North
Korean People's Army
North Korean People's
Army (NKPA)
and atrocities, 61, 63,
82
and casualties, 43, 50,
52, 59, 61, 63, 65,
75, 82, 86-87, 93,
108, 112

and Chochiwon, 44
and Chonan, 43
and crossing over 38th
    parallel and invad-
    ing ROK, 12-17,
    29, 31-34
diminished strength
    of, 50-52
and early clashes on
    38th parallel, 29
and Inchon invasion,
    40, 65, 67-79
and Osan, 41-43
and Pusan (Naktong)
    Perimeter, 47, 49-
    61, 63-65
and Pyongtaek, 43
ROKA superior to,
    13-14
and Seoul, 35, 36, 81-
    93
and Soviet backing,
    15, 29, 31, 42, 58,
    63, 82
strategy of, 38, 50
and Taejon, 45
and UN resolution on
    attack as breach of
    world peace, 34
Notch, 53

Obong-ni Ridge (No-
    Name Ridge), 57-58,
    63
Observatory Hill, 78
Ongjin Peninsula, 32
Operation Blueheart,
    36
Operation Chromite,
    69-77, 84, 92
Osan, 40, 41-43
Outer Mongolia
    (Mongolian People's
    Republic), 20

Owen, Joseph R.,
    101

Paik Sun Yup, 59-60,
    61
Palmi-do, 74
Panmunjom, 112
Peng Dehuai, 98
Perry, Miller O., 41,
    42
Poats, Rutherford, 90
Pohang (P'ohang), 32,
    45, 51, 63
Poland, 20
Port Arthur (Lüshun),
    20
Potsdam Conference,
    22
Puller, Chesty, 76, 77,
    81, 83, 84, 85, 90-92,
    100, 106
Pusan (Naktong)
    Perimeter, 38, 39, 40,
    45, 47, 49-61, 51, 60,
    63-65, 109
Pyongtaek, 41, 43
Pyongyang (P'y-
    ongyang), 32, 96, 98,
    99, 105

Radio Hill, 74
Red Beach, 73, 76-77
Regimental Combat
    Team (RCT), 37
Republic of (South)
    Korea (ROK)
    creation of, 28, 29
    and NKPA crossing
        38th parallel and
        invading ROK,
        12-17, 29, 31-32
    and Seoul, 35, 36
    and unification of two
        Koreas, 97

and U.S. backing, 29
and withdrawal of
    U.S. troops, 29
See also Republic of
    (South) Korea
    Army
Republic of (South)
    Korea Army (ROKA)
    and aggressive action
        north of 38th paral-
        lel, 98-99
    and casualties, 61, 93,
        112
    and China, 100
    diminished strength
        of, 38
    and Inchon invasion,
        72, 81, 82
    and Pusan (Naktong)
        Perimeter, 50, 51,
        59-60, 61, 63
    and reunification of
        two Koreas, 97
    and Seoul, 83, 86, 89,
        93
    as superior to NKPA,
        13-14
    Walker as commander
        of, 44-45
Rhee, Syngman, 12, 28,
    38, 60, 92, 97
Ridgway, Matthew B.,
    93, 115
Rochester, U.S.S., 74
Roise, Harold S., 57-58
ROK. See Republic of
    (South) Korea
ROKA. See Republic of
    (South) Korea Army
ROK Capital Division,
    98-99
ROK 1st Corps, 97, 100
ROK 1st Division, 59-60,
    61, 99, 100

ROK 3rd Division, 63, 97
ROK 6th Division, 99
ROK 8th Division, 63
ROK 10th Division, 60
Roosevelt, Franklin D.
  and Cairo Conference, 21, 26
  death of, 22
  and Yalta Conference, 20-21, 26
Rusk, Dean, 23-24
Russo-Japanese War of 1904-1905, 20

Sachon (Sach'on), 53, 55-56
Sakhalin Peninsula, 20
Samchok, 32
Scott, Win, 102
Scully, Pat, 106
Seoul, 81-93
  and falling to NPKA, 35, 36
  and Inchon invasion, 68, 73, 76, 78
  as key to victory, 68
  liberation of, 85, 87, 89, 92
  and 38th parallel, 24, 25, 31
Shepherd, Lemuel C. Jr., 68-69, 83
Sherman, Forrest P., 70, 71
Smith, Charles B. "Brad," 39, 40, 41-42
Smith, H.J., 87
Smith, N. Harry, 108
Smith, Oliver P., 71, 81, 84, 85, 100, 103, 105-106, 107, 108
Southern Manchurian Railroad, 20

South Korea. See Republic of (South) Korea (ROK)
Soviet Union
  and borders with Korea, 25
  and China, 20, 23
  Chinese and North Koreans fighting for, 36-37
  and Cold War, 20-22, 27
  and creation of DPRK, 28-29
  and division of Korea, 26-28
  entry into World War II against Japan, 20-21, 22, 23
  and establishment of 38th parallel, 23-25, 26
  and Korea as puppet state, 21-22, 28-29
  and Manchuria, 20, 23
  NKPA backed by, 15, 29, 31, 42, 58, 63, 82
  and Potsdam Conference, 22
  and withdrawal north of 38th parallel, 26
  and withdrawal of troops from DPRK, 29
  and Yalta Conference, 20-21, 23, 26
Sowolmi-do, 69
Stalin, Joseph
  and China, 20-21, 23
  and Korea as puppet state, 21-22, 28-29
  and Potsdam Conference, 22

  and U.S. dropping atomic bombs on Hiroshima and Nagasaki, 23
  and U.S. testing atomic bomb, 22
  and Yalta Conference, 20-21, 23, 26
"stand or die" order, and Walker, 45-46
State-War-Navy (departments) Coordinating Committee, 23
Stephens, Richard W., 39
Struble, Arthur D., 72, 74, 75, 77-78, 84
Sudong-ni, 100, 101
Sung Shih-lun, 102
Suny, Gregor, 23
Sutter, Allan, 78
Suwon, 36, 40

Tabu-dong corridor, 60, 61
Taebaek Mountains, 25, 83, 100
Taegu, 44, 51, 56, 59, 60
Taejon, 40, 43, 45, 83
Taft, Robert A., 37-38
Taplett, Robert D., 55, 58, 74, 75, 76
Task Force Drysdale, 106
Task Force Hill, 57
Task Force Kean, 52, 53-54, 55
Task Force Seven, 84
38th parallel
  and climate, 25, 102
  and defensive problems, 24
  and division of Korea, 26-28

early clashes along, 29
and economic prob-
lems, 25
and end of Korean
War, 112
establishment of, 23-
25, 26
military actions north
of, 96
and NKPA crossing
and invading
ROK, 12-17, 29,
31-34
Toktong Pass, 102, 103,
106
Toland, John, 26
Tosan, 55
Treaty of Friendship
and Alliance, 23
Truman, Harry, 33
and China, 34, 98
and China and North
Korea fighting for
Soviet Union, 36-37
and division of Korea,
27-28
and Inchon invasion,
73
and intervention in
Korea, 33-38
and MacArthur as
head of UN Com-
mand, 44
and NKPA crossing
38th parallel, 14, 33
and Potsdam Confer-
ence, 22
and ROK Army, 29
and U.S. air and naval
operations south
of 38th parallel
against NKPA,
34, 37
See also United States

T-34 tanks, 15, 31, 42, 58,
63, 82
Tumen River, 25

Uijongbu, 92
United Nations Com-
mand (UNC)
and aggressive action
north of 38th paral-
lel, 96
and casualties, 112
and Chosin, 95-103,
105-109
establishment of, 43-
44
and Inchon invasion,
65, 67-79, 93
and Pusan (Naktong)
Perimeter, 47, 49-
61, 63-65
and Seoul, 81-93
strength of, 50-51
United Nations, found-
ing of, 20
United Nations (UN)
Security Council
and aggressive action
north of 38th paral-
lel, 96, 98
and Chinese interven-
tion, 100
and division of Korea,
28
and DPRK ending
aggression and
recalling NKPA,
33, 34
and NKPA's attack as
breach of world
peace, 34
and United States as
executive agent and
organizer of UN
Command, 43-44

United States
and aggressive action
north of 38th paral-
lel, 96
and Cairo Conference,
21, 26
and casualties, 43, 45,
46, 55, 58, 59, 65,
75, 79, 83, 86-87,
92-93, 106, 108, 112
and China, 34
and Chonan, 43
and Chosin, 95-103,
105-109
and Cold War, 20-22,
27
and division of Korea,
27-28
and establishment of
38th parallel, 23-25,
26
and first ground
forces in Korea,
39-41
and Inchon invasion,
65, 67-79, 93
and intervention in
Korea, 33-38
and MacArthur's
display of strength,
38-39
NKPA backed by, 29
and NKPA crossing
38th parallel, 12-14,
32-34
and Osan, 40, 41-43
and Potsdam Confer-
ence, 22
and Pusan (Naktong)
Perimeter, 47, 49-
61, 63-65
and Pyongtaek, 43
and ROKA superior
to NKPA, 13-14

and Seoul, 81-93
strategy of, 38
and Taejon, 45
and troops moving to
ROK, 39-41, 43,
44-45, 46-47, 52-53,
68-69, 71-72, 82
and UN request to act
as executive agent
and organizer of
UN Command, 43-
44
and UN resolution on
NPKA attack as
breach of world
peace, 34
and withdrawal of
troops from ROK,
29
and Yalta Conference,
20, 26
See also Truman,
Harry
U.S. 1st Battalion, 39, 40,
108
U.S. 1st Cavalry Division,
44, 45, 50, 61, 89, 92,
98, 99, 100
U.S. 1st Corps, 98
U.S. 1st Marine Division,
68-69, 81, 82, 83, 84,
86, 90, 92-93, 98, 99,
100, 103, 106, 108,
109
U.S. 1st Marine Provi-
sional Brigade, 46-47,
52-53, 65
U.S. Korea Military
Advisory Group, 13,
29
U.S. 2nd Battalion, 54,
57-58
U.S. 2nd Infantry Division,
46, 60, 63, 105

U.S. 3rd Battalion, 40, 55,
58
U.S. 3rd Infantry Division,
101, 108
U.S. 5th Air Force, 52
U.S. 5th Cavalry Regiment,
61
U.S. 5th Marines, 55, 57-
58, 63, 81-82, 84, 86,
90, 103, 106-107
U.S. 5th Regimental
Combat Team (RCT),
46, 52, 53, 54
U.S. 7th Cavalry Regiment,
89
U.S. 7th Fleet, 34
U.S. 7th Infantry Division,
84, 86, 89, 93, 98, 99,
101
U.S. 7th Marines, 86, 90,
101, 102, 103, 106-107,
108
U.S. 8th Army, 39, 44-46,
70, 73, 83-84, 87, 89,
96, 98, 102, 105, 108,
109
U.S. 8th Cavalry Regiment,
100
U.S. 9th Infantry Division,
58
U.S. 10th Corps, 81-82,
84, 89, 96, 98, 99, 102,
105, 108
U.S. 10th Corps Head-
quarters (HQ), 71-77
U.S. 11th Marines, 90
U.S. 17th Infantry Regi-
ment, 101
U.S. 19th Infantry Divi-
sion, 58
U.S. 21st Infantry Divi-
sion, 39
U.S. 21st Regiment, 40, 44
U.S. 23rd Regiment, 60

U.S. 24th Infantry Divi-
sion (Task Force
Smith), 12-13, 39-43,
45, 50, 52, 53, 56, 59
U.S. 24th Regiment, 53
U.S. 25th Infantry Divi-
sion, 44, 50, 52, 60
U.S. 27th "Wolfhound"
Regiment, 60, 61
U.S. 29th Regimental
Combat Team, 44
U.S. 31st Infantry
Division, 89
U.S. 32nd Infantry
Division, 84, 87
U.S. 32nd Infantry
Regiment, 84, 86, 89
U.S. 34th Regiment, 43
U.S. 35th Infantry
Regiment, 52, 53
U.S. 52nd Field Artillery
Battalion, 41
Unsan, 100

Waegwan, 50, 51, 61,
83
Wae Pang, 52, 53
Walker, Walton H., 39
and breakout, 70, 83-
84, 87
and China, 102, 105
and command of U.S.
and ROK ground
forces in Korea,
44-45
and Inchon invasion,
73
and military opera-
tions north of 38th
parallel, 96
and Pusan (Naktong)
Perimeter, 47, 50,
51, 53, 56, 57, 58,
60, 63, 64-65

and Seoul, 83-84
and "stand or die"
    order, 45-46
and Taejon, 45
and Task Force Kean,
    52
and U.S. 8th Army, 39,
    44-46, 70, 73, 83-84,
    87, 89, 96, 98, 102,
    105, 108, 109
Wolmi-do, 69, 73-74,
    76
Wonju, 32
Wonsan, 93, 96, 97, 98,
    99

World War II
    and defeat of Germany,
        22
    and entry of Soviet
        Union against
        Japan, 20-21, 22, 23
    and Japanese surren-
        der, 19, 23, 24
    and struggle for
        world domination,
        19-23
    and U.S. dropping
        atomic bombs on
        Hiroshima and
        Nagasaki, 23

Wyrick, William, 42

Xue Litai, 22

Yadam-ni, 102, 103, 105,
    106
Yalta Conference, 20-21,
    23, 26
Yalu River, 12, 25, 97,
    98, 99, 101
Yancey, John, 103
Yellow Sea, 15, 25, 68,
    69
Yongdok, 32
Yongdung-p'o, 82, 83, 84

page:

10: Courtesy of the United Nations
15: Courtesy of the National Archives Central Plains Region
18: Courtesy of the Library of Congress, LC-USZ62-17977
21: Courtesy of the National Archives
27: © Bettmann/CORBIS
30: © CORBIS
35: © Bettmann/CORBIS
41: © Associated Press, AP
44: Department of Defense, Courtesy of the Harry S. Truman Library
48: © Associated Press, AP
54: © Bettmann/CORBIS
59: © Hulton-Deutsch Collection/ CORBIS

62: Department of Defense, Courtesy of the Harry S. Truman Library
66: Courtesy of the National Archives
75: Courtesy of the National Archives
78: Courtesy of the National Archives
80: © Hulton/Archive, Getty Images
86: © Associated Press, AP
91: © Associated Press, AP
94: © Associated Press, AP
99: Copyright unknown/Courtesy of the Harry S. Truman Library
104: Courtesy of the National Archives
107: © Associated Press, AP
110: Courtesy of the United Nations
113: Courtesy of the United Nations

Cover: © Hulton-Deutsch Collection/CORBIS
Frontis: Courtesy of the Library of Congress, Geography and Map Division

Earle Rice Jr., is a former senior design engineer and technical writer in the aerospace industry. After serving nine years with the U.S. Marine Corps—including a tour of combat duty in Korea as a machine-gun squad leader—he attended San Jose City College and Foothill College on the San Francisco peninsula. He has been devoted full-time to his writing since 1993 and has written more than 40 books for young adults. Earle is a member of the Society of Children's Book Writers and Illustrators, the League of World War I Aviation Historians and its British sister organization, Cross & Cockade International, the United States Naval Institute, the Air Force Association, and the Disabled American Veterans.

Caspar W. Weinberger was the fifteenth secretary of defense, serving under President Ronald Reagan from 1981 to 1987. Born in California in 1917, he fought in the Pacific during World War II then went on to pursue a law career. He became an active member of the California Republican Party and was named the party's chairman in 1962. Over the next decade, Weinberger held several federal government offices, including chairman of the Federal Trade Commission and secretary of health, education, and welfare. Ronald Reagan appointed him to be secretary of defense in 1981. He became one of the most respected secretaries of defense in history and served longer than any previous secretary except for Robert McNamara (who served 1961–1968). Today, Weinberger is chairman of the influential *Forbes* magazine.